The SOUTHFORK™ RANCH Cookbook

The SOUTHFORK™ RANCH Cookbook

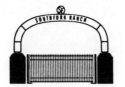

Bea Terry

WILLIAM MORROW AND COMPANY, INC.
New York 1982

Library of Congress Cataloging in Publication Data

Terry, Bea.
Southfork Ranch Cookbook.

Includes index.
1. Cookery, American--Texas. I. Title.
TX715.T35924 641.5 81-16993
ISBN 0-688-01000-8 AACR2

Printed in the United States of America

First Edition

1 2 3 4 5 6 7 8 9 10

BOOK DESIGN BY MICHAEL MAUCERI
DRAWINGS BY HONI WERNER

TO
DOROTHY

my beloved sister
and
my best friend

CONTENTS

INTRODUCTION

The Southfork™ Ranch is dwarfed in area by hundreds of other Texas spreads. But what this 200-acre piece of earth lacks in size is more than compensated for in celebrity. No one would dare wager against its being the most well-known, best-loved rural spot anywhere in the world where there are television sets. It has been designated the number-one tourist attraction in the greater Dallas/Fort Worth area.

The main house appears to be a living entity as it stands imposingly on its quarter section, some distance from the public road. It seems to know that it is the second best-known manse in the land—that is, if one counts the White House as number one.

The ranch became a "star" almost overnight after the location managers for Lorimar Productions of California decided in 1978 to use it for the prime-time TV show that became an international household word—DALLAS™. After that, things were never quite the same again at the real-life Southfork.

Each day now, hundreds of cars line the side of the road in front of the main house. There are license plates from all over the United States and Canada. If you tarry a spell at the trading post, you might talk to visitors from many foreign lands—Australia, the Orient, the Middle East, Europe, the Philippines, England, Africa, and other countries and continents. They come to take pictures and to stare. When they talk, it is in quiet, respectful tones, perhaps because of that odd sense of surprise people have when they see a star is a real person. There it is, this expansive two-story house, as big as life, actually standing there.

The ranch house was built in 1971 by its owner, Joe Rand Duncan, a Dallas real-estate developer, who goes right on living there with his wife and family. He purchased the land in 1970, drew his own plans for all the main buildings, and spent two years converting the cotton and wheat fields into a Quarter horse ranch; television wasn't what he had in mind at the time. And the ranch goes right on operating, too. Even from outside the gate it's a fine panorama, enhanced by the beautiful race horses that prance and cavort regally or stand together nuzzling in the open pasture. Here and there a mare nurses her colt. A pair of donkeys and a couple of buffalo pay no attention to their famous surroundings and graze matter-of-factly on the Bermuda grass.

When Lorimar Productions shoots on location at Southfork nowadays and the film crew is all over the place, the big house is a pleasant retreat for the stars who play the Ewing™ family members on the show—a place to sip a glass of iced tea, read a script, knit, or play the piano while they wait for calls to the set outside for shooting. It did not begin that way; most of the filming for DALLAS used to be done in California. But as time went on, more and more was done in Texas, at Southfork and all around, including Dallas. (The state of Texas now ranks number three in movie making, only behind California and New York.)

Periodically, the production crews and the actors all pack up and go back to California to shoot the interior scenes for the show, and things quiet down a bit at Southfork, but not all that much. The well-known gate to the ranch is always closed on weekends, but Mondays through Fridays fans are allowed some one hundred yards inside the grounds, down the asphalt road to the trading post, to get a closer look, to say they've "been to Southfork," and to buy a variety of souvenirs and cool soft drinks. If people venture farther down the road toward the house, they are promptly turned back by a guard—that is, unless they take a paid tour of the premises. For a higher tour fee, they can even come on in on days when Lorimar Productions is shooting scenes from DALLAS and maybe catch a glimpse of the actors they know so well on their TV screens.

The Southfork Ranch is easy to get to, only thirty miles from Dallas. Several companies operate tour buses to the ranch, and any travel agent in the city will gladly answer queries about such tours. To get there by car, drive north from Dallas on U.S. 75 to Exit 30/Parker Road at Plano. Drive east on Parker Road for six miles to the intersection of FM-2551. Turn right to the entrance. Of course, no cars are allowed inside the gate without special authorization—only for those who have business there. Nobody minds that. In fact, thousands upon thousands of tourists fly in to the Dallas/Fort Worth airport, rent a car, and drive eagerly to see the Southfork spread.

And that's not all. One may rent a party site on the grounds; a huge tent will be hoisted for private entertaining—for a price. The real-life Southfork Ranch has become the "in" place for prestigious folks to toss their parties. In the future, there will be a permanent building that can be leased for such purposes.

But after all is said and done, Southfork is just home to the Duncans. They watch TV like other people, though unlike anyone else, they do see their own home on the screen while sitting inside that same house, both at once. But they sleep here, cook and eat here just like any real-life Texans would. Not everybody outside of Texas understands about Texas food. So now the Southfork Ranch has its own cookbook with the kind of indigenous recipes that people really use around here, the kind of food the Duncan family cooks and enjoys. They figure if the Ewing family really lived here, this is what they would have on the dinner table, too.

About the Author

Bea Terry was raised twenty miles as the crow flies from where Joe Rand Duncan would one day build the Southfork™ Ranch. She started to cook when she was eight years old, the real home cooking of North Texas, learning from her mother, from watching other cooks, and from her father, too, who was as good as anybody around at making beef stew, fried chicken, and chicken-fried steak. She really started earlier than that—she recalls making her first cream gravy when she was seven!

Miss Terry lived in Hollywood for twenty-five years, where she maintained her own public-relations office, representing personalities in the world of entertainment—radio, motion pictures, television, and recording. She was involved in promoting many songs to the top of the hit parade and in guiding unknowns to stardom. But she never stopped cooking; far from it. Entertaining was an important part of her business and she became one of the best at cooking for a crowd. It wasn't all Texas cooking in those days. She added her own gourmet dishes to the file of recipes she had started as a teenager and someday will make another cookbook out of the hundreds she has created.

A few years ago, Miss Terry went back to Texas and now lives in Waco. But, once in show business, always in show business—naturally she got to know her fellow Texan "J.R." Duncan at the Southfork Ranch of television fame. And naturally, they talked about the Texas food they both grew up with and how they really have the same food at home today. The cookstoves are more up to date, so are a lot of the recipes, and Miss Bea has learned a lot about interesting seasonings over the years. But basically, it's the same cooking, and so she went back into those precious files and made this book for Southfork and for all the people everywhere who have never realized that Texas cooks are some of the best in the U.S.A.

BREADS

FLAKY BISCUITS

2 cups all-purpose flour
4 tsps double-acting baking powder
¾ tsp salt
1 tsp sugar
½ tsp cream of tartar
½ cup vegetable shortening (not oil)
⅔ cup cold milk

Sift dry ingredients into mixing bowl. Using a pastry blender, cut in shortening until mixture is like coarse crumbs. Do not overmix. Add cold milk and stir with a fork until dry ingredients are dampened.

Turn dough onto lightly floured surface. Spread by patting to ½-inch thickness. Cut with floured biscuit cutter and place on ungreased baking sheet.

Bake in oven preheated to 425° for 10–12 minutes or until golden brown. Makes 12 to 16 medium-size biscuits.

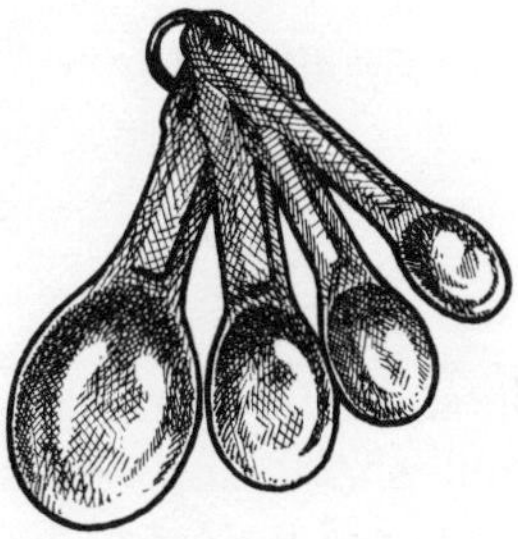

SOUR CREAM BISCUITS

2 cups all-purpose flour
1 Tbsp double-acting baking powder
½ tsp soda
½ tsp salt
¾ cup dairy sour cream
2 Tbsps milk
2 Tbsps cooking oil
melted butter

Sift dry ingredients together into a mixing bowl. Mix sour cream, milk and cooking oil together. Add sour cream mixture to dry ingredients. Mix well. Turn onto sparsely floured surface. Knead lightly.

Spread dough by patting to ½-inch thickness. Cut with floured biscuit cutter and place on greased baking sheet. Brush tops with melted butter. Bake in oven preheated to 425° for 12–15 minutes or until golden brown. Makes 12 to 16 medium-size biscuits.

COUNTRY LIGHT BREAD

2 cups milk
1 tsp salt
2 Tbsps vegetable shortening (not oil)
2 Tbsps sugar
2 cakes yeast
5⅓ cups all-purpose flour

Combine milk, salt, shortening and sugar in a saucepan. Place over medium heat until shortening melts and steaming starts. Remove from burner and cool to tepid.

Finely crumble yeast into milk mixture. Stir until yeast is dissolved. Add ½ of the flour and beat until smooth. Gradually add remaining flour, mixing after each addition.

Lightly flour a bread board and turn out dough on board. Knead until smooth. Place in large greased mixing bowl. Brush oil over top of dough. Cover and let rise approximately 1½ hours or until dough doubles in size.

Punch down dough with fist until it is its original size. Divide dough into equal parts. Shape each into oblong rolls. Place each in a separate 9x5x3-inch greased loaf pan. Cover and allow to rise until doubled in size, about 1 hour.

Place pans on middle shelf in oven with about 1-inch space between the pans. Bake in oven preheated to 400° for 50 minutes. Serve hot, with butter.

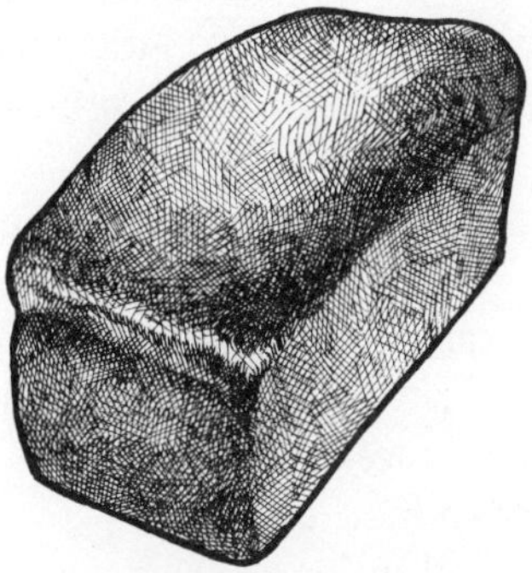

HUSH PUPPIES

2 cups yellow cornmeal
3 Tbsps flour
1 tsp salt
1 tsp sugar
1 tsp double-acting baking powder
¾ tsp baking soda
½ tsp chili powder
2 eggs, beaten
⅔ cup buttermilk
2 Tbsps finely minced onion
oil for frying

Sift dry ingredients together into a mixing bowl. Add eggs, buttermilk, and minced onion, stirring until smooth.

Drop a level tablespoon of mixture at a time into hot deep fat. Cook a few at a time until golden brown. Drain on absorbent paper. Serves 4 to 6.

MEXI CORN BREAD

- ⅓ cup all-purpose flour
- 1 tsp salt
- 1 tsp double-acting baking powder
- ½ tsp baking soda
- 1 tsp chili powder
- 2 Tbsps sugar
- 1 cup yellow cornmeal (preferably stone-ground)
- 1 cup buttermilk
- 1 Tbsp bacon drippings, cooled
- 2 eggs
- ¼ cup chopped pimiento
- ¼ cup crumbled crisp fried bacon
- 2 Tbsps finely minced onion
- 1 cup canned whole-kernel corn, drained
- 3 Tbsps cooking oil

Preheat oven to 425°. Sift premeasured flour, salt, baking powder, baking soda and chili powder together into a mixing bowl. Add sugar and cornmeal. Mix thoroughly.

Add buttermilk, bacon drippings and eggs. Mix well. Stir in pimiento, crumbled bacon, onion and corn, distributing well. Pour oil into a heavy iron skillet. Heat over medium heat until sizzling. Turn off burner.

Spoon batter into hot skillet. Carefully place in preheated oven. Bake for 25 minutes or until golden brown.

CHEESY CORN SPOON BREAD

- 1 cup yellow cornmeal
- ¼ cup flour
- 1 tsp double-acting baking powder
- 1 Tbsp sugar
- 1¾ cups milk (save ½ cup for last step of recipe)
- 2 eggs
- ¼ cup grated American cheese
- 3 Tbsps bacon drippings

Sift dry ingredients together into a mixing bowl. In another bowl, beat 1¼ cups of the milk with eggs. Pour mixture into dry ingredients. Mix to dampen. Fold in cheese, blending well.

Spread bacon fat over bottom of a medium-size iron skillet. Spoon batter into skillet, spreading evenly with spoon. Pour remaining ½ cup of milk over batter.

Bake in oven preheated to 400° for 35 minutes. Spoon onto plates.

CORN STICKS

- 1½ cups coarse-ground yellow cornmeal
- ¼ cup cooking oil
- ¾ cup boiling water
- 2 eggs, well beaten
- ¾ cup buttermilk
- 2½ tsps double-acting baking powder
- ½ tsp baking soda
- ½ tsp salt
- 1 Tbsp sugar
- ¾ cup flour

In a mixing bowl, combine cornmeal, oil and boiling water. Stir until thick and smooth. Add beaten eggs and milk. Blend well.

Sift dry ingredients together and add to cornmeal mixture. Blend thoroughly with spoon.

Brush 2 iron corn stick pans with oil. Place pans in oven preheated to 375°. When pans are hot, remove from oven and spoon batter into each cup almost to the rims.

Bake for 25–30 minutes or until golden brown. Makes 14 sticks.

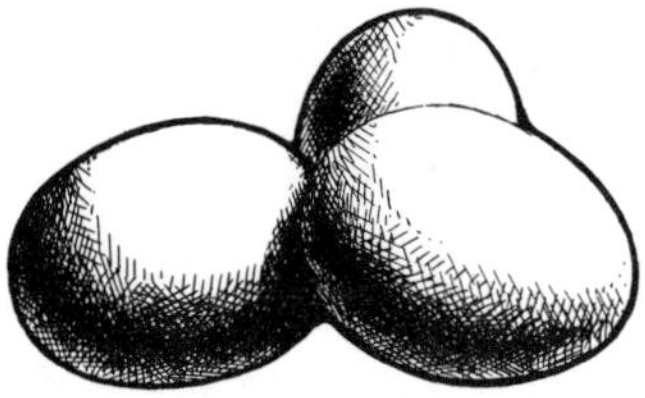

JALAPEÑO CORN BREAD

- ⅔ cup flour
- 1 tsp sugar
- 1 tsp salt
- 3 tsps double-acting baking powder
- 1 tsp baking soda
- 1⅔ cups yellow cornmeal (preferably stone-ground)
- 2 eggs
- 1 cup buttermilk
- ¼ cup vegetable oil
- One 4-oz can chopped jalapeño peppers, well drained
- 2 Tbsps dry onion soup mix
- 3 slices crisp fried bacon, crumbled
- 3 Tbsps bacon drippings

Preheat oven to 425°. Sift all dry ingredients together except cornmeal and soup mix. After sifting, add cornmeal and stir with a spoon.

Beat eggs, buttermilk and oil together in a mixing bowl. Add dry ingredients and stir until smooth. Add drained peppers, soup mix and crumbled bacon. Stir until ingredients are evenly distributed.

Place medium-size iron skillet over medium heat on top of stove. Add bacon drippings, spread over bottom of pan. When hot, take from burner. Turn batter into the hot skillet.

Bake in preheated oven for 25 minutes until well browned and solid in center. Cut into 6 wedges and serve hot.

ONION-CHEESE BREAD

1 egg
½ cup buttermilk
1½ cups biscuit mix
2 Tbsps dry onion soup mix
¾ cup shredded Cheddar cheese
2 Tbsps melted butter
2 Tbsps shredded Cheddar cheese (for top)
1 Tbsp dry onion soup mix (for top)

Grease the inside of a 9-inch-round cake pan and set aside. Beat egg and buttermilk together until frothy. Place biscuit mix in a bowl. Stir in egg mixture and blend well with a spoon. Add soup mix and shredded cheese. Combine well.

Spread dough in pan. Spoon melted butter evenly on top. Sprinkle cheese and soup mix on top. Bake in oven preheated to 375° for 20 minutes or until golden brown. Cut into wedges and serve hot. Makes 6 to 8 wedges.

COTTAGE SPOON BREAD

1¾ cups milk
½ cup cornmeal
1 tsp salt
2 tsps sugar
3 egg yolks, beaten
3 Tbsps butter, melted
1 cup small-curd cottage cheese
1 tsp finely snipped chives
3 Tbsps finely grated green pepper
2 tsps grated onion
3 egg whites
melted butter

Heat milk in a large saucepan to scalding. Add cornmeal, salt and sugar. Cook, stirring constantly until thickened. Blend small amount of the hot cornmeal mixture with the beaten egg yolks. Add egg yolk mixture to saucepan, mixing thoroughly.

Add melted butter, cottage cheese, chives, green pepper and onion to pan. Stir well. Remove from heat. Beat egg whites until stiff but not dry. Gradually fold meal mixture into egg whites.

Spoon into a large greased casserole. Bake in oven preheated to 375° for 35–40 minutes. Serve at once with melted butter. Serves 4 to 6.

HOE CAKES

1½ cups coarse-ground yellow cornmeal
¼ cup flour
1 tsp salt
½ tsp double-acting baking powder
1½ cups boiling water

3 Tbsps bacon grease
¼ cup milk
meat fat, butter or margarine for frying

Combine cornmeal, flour, salt and baking powder in a bowl. Add boiling water and bacon grease, stirring vigorously until thoroughly mixed. Add milk and stir until smooth.

Heat greased griddle. Drop 2 heaping tablespoons to a cake onto griddle; cook until undersides are golden. Turn and pat down each cake with a pancake turner. Cook until golden. Grease griddle as more cakes are made.

Serve hot with butter. Makes 12 to 18 hoe cakes.

SAUSAGE PANCAKES

6 cooked sausage patties or links
1½ cups flour
1½ tsps double-acting baking powder
½ tsp baking soda
1 tsp salt
1 Tbsp sugar
2 eggs
1½ cups buttermilk
3 Tbsps cooking oil

Cut cooked sausage into small pieces. Sift all dry ingredients together.

Combine eggs, buttermilk and oil in a mixing bowl. Beat until well mixed. Add dry ingredients and stir until just blended. Add sausage and stir.

Heat lightly greased griddle over medium heat until drop of water sprinkled on it sizzles and dances. Spoon 2 or 3 tablespoons of batter for each pancake onto griddle. Bake until edges are brown, turn and cook other side.

Serve hot with syrup, jam or jelly. Batter may be used for waffles. Makes 14 to 16 pancakes.

CHEESY POPOVERS

3 eggs
3 Tbsps cooking oil
½ tsp salt
1 cup milk
1 cup all-purpose flour, sifted
2 Tbsps grated American cheese

Preheat oven to 400°. Use a muffin pan with 12 large cups. Grease the inside of each cup with cooking oil.

Combine eggs, oil, salt and milk in a mixing bowl. Beat on low speed with an electric mixer until well blended. Add the flour and beat just until the batter is smooth. Remove the mixer.

With a tablespoon, stir in the cheese and mix well. Fill each muffin cup ½ full of batter. Bake in preheated oven for 20–25 minutes or until golden brown. Serve hot. Makes 12 popovers.

SPICY APPLE GEMS

1 egg
¾ cup milk
¼ cup melted butter or margarine
2 cups all-purpose flour
½ cup sugar
1 Tbsp double-acting baking powder

½ tsp salt
1 tsp cinnamon
1 cup (packed) coarsely grated apple
¼ cup chopped nuts or raisins

Beat egg and milk with an electric mixer in a small mixing bowl. Add melted butter and beat for 1 minute.

Sift flour, sugar, baking powder, salt and cinnamon together in a large mixing bowl. Stir in apples and nuts or raisins. Pour in milk mixture and stir just until most of dry ingredients are moistened. Do not overmix as batter should be lumpy.

Spoon into greased muffin cups until each is ⅔ filled. Bake in oven preheated to 400° for 20–25 minutes or until golden brown. Makes 12 muffins.

PEANUT BUTTER MUFFINS

¾ cup milk
½ cup honey
3 Tbsp cooking oil
½ cup chunky peanut butter
1 egg
2 cups self-rising flour

Preheat oven to 425°. Grease the inside of 12 large muffin cups with cooking oil.

In a mixing bowl, blend the milk, honey, cooking oil, peanut butter and egg with an electric mixer on low speed until well mixed. With a spoon, stir in the self-rising flour until mixed but not overbeaten.

Spoon batter into the muffin cups until each is about ¾ full. Bake for 20 minutes until golden. Makes 12 large muffins.

APPLE BUTTER MUFFINS

½ cup milk
¼ cup cooking oil
½ cup apple butter
1 egg
4 Tbsps honey
2 cups self-rising flour

Preheat oven to 425°. Grease inside of 12 muffin cups.

Combine milk, cooking oil, apple butter, egg and honey in a medium-size bowl. Blend with an electric mixer on low speed until well mixed. Add self-rising flour and beat at low speed until flour is mixed in and large lumps are gone.

Spoon into muffin cups until each cup is about ¾ full. Bake for 20–25 minutes or until toothpick inserted into the center of a muffin comes out clean. Allow muffins to remain in pan for a minute or two before removing. Serve warm. Makes 12 large muffins.

PRUNE BRAN MUFFINS

2 cups whole-wheat flour
1 Tbsp double-acting baking powder
½ tsp salt
¼ cup sugar
1 cup milk
1 egg
¼ cup cooking oil
½ cup finely chopped pitted prunes

Preheat oven to 425°. Grease inside of 12 muffin cups.

Sift flour and baking powder together in a mixing bowl. Stir in salt and sugar.

Add milk, egg and oil. Blend with an electric mixer on low speed until mixed but not over-beaten. Add prunes and stir into batter.

Spoon batter into cups until each is ¾ full. Bake for 20–25 minutes until golden. Allow muffins to stay in pan for a minute or two before removing. Serve warm with butter. Makes 12 large muffins.

BANANA NUT BREAD

½ cup cooking oil
2 eggs
¾ cup sugar
1½ cups mashed ripe bananas
¼ cup milk
2½ cups bran flakes cereal
2 cups flour
1 tsp double-acting baking powder
½ tsp soda
½ tsp salt
½ cup chopped nuts

Combine oil, eggs, sugar, bananas and milk in a mixing bowl. Beat with a spoon until well mixed. Stir in bran flakes. Mix well. Cover and set aside for 10–15 minutes.

Sift dry ingredients together and stir in nuts. Add to banana mixture in bowl. Mix well with spoon.

Turn batter into a greased 9x5x3-inch loaf pan. Bake in oven preheated to 350° for 1 hour or until toothpick inserted in center of loaf comes out clean. Cool for 15 minutes before turning out of pan.

PUMPKIN BREAD

- ⅓ cup seedless raisins
- ⅓ cup cooking oil
- 1 cup light brown sugar
- ⅓ cup molasses
- 2 Tbsps sherry
- 2 eggs
- 1 cup mashed cooked or canned pumpkin
- 1⅔ cups all-purpose flour, unsifted
- ½ tsp cinnamon
- ¼ tsp allspice
- ¼ tsp nutmeg
- ½ tsp baking soda
- ½ tsp double-acting baking powder
- 1 tsp salt
- 1 cup chopped nuts

Cover raisins with hot water and let soak for 1 hour. Drain, then dry with paper towels. Preheat oven to 350°. Grease and flour inside of a 9x5x3-inch loaf pan. Set aside.

Combine cooking oil, sugar, molasses, sherry and eggs in a mixing bowl. Beat with electric mixer at medium speed until well blended and frothy. Add pumpkin and mix well with a spoon.

Sift flour, spices, soda, baking powder and salt together. Gradually beat dry ingredients into the oil mixture. Add raisins and nuts, blending well with a spoon.

Spread batter in prepared pan and bake in preheated oven for 1 hour or until wooden toothpick inserted in the center comes out clean. Allow bread to cool for 10 minutes in pan. Turn onto a rack and finish cooling.

CARROT BREAD

1½ cups flour
1 tsp baking soda
1 tsp double-acting baking powder
½ tsp salt
1 tsp cinnamon
1 cup sugar
2 eggs
¾ cup corn oil
1 cup grated raw carrots
½ cup chopped nuts

Preheat oven to 350°. Grease inside of a 9x5x3-inch loaf pan. Place 2 tablespoons flour in pan and shake to coat inside. Shake out and discard loose flour.

Sift and measure flour. Add soda, baking powder, salt and cinnamon. Sift together into a mixing bowl. Stir in sugar.

Place eggs in a cup and beat with fork until mixed and creamy. Add eggs and oil to flour mixture and stir with a spoon until well mixed. Add grated carrots and stir until distributed evenly. Fold in nuts.

Place batter in prepared oven. Bake in preheated oven for 1 hour. Allow bread to cool in pan for 10 minutes. Remove from pan and finish cooling on a cake rack.

SOUPS

SPLIT PEA SOUP

1-lb package dried green split peas
1 tsp salt
½ cup chopped fat from ham
water as directed
1 cup chopped celery and leaves
2 medium carrots, peeled and thinly sliced
1 medium onion, chopped
½ tsp seasoned salt
⅛ tsp pepper
dash garlic powder
1½ cups cubed cooked lean ham

Rinse peas in a colander under running water. Place in 6-quart pot. Add salt, ham fat and 8 cups boiling water. Place over high heat and bring to a rolling boil. Reduce heat to medium. Stir peas occasionally as they cook. When tender put through strainer to remove outer husks. Return to large pot.

Combine celery, carrots, onion and seasonings in a 2½-quart saucepan. Add 2 cups boiling water. Cook until vegetables are almost tender. Add ham and cook until vegetables are very tender.

Add vegetable/ham mixture to peas. Stir well. If a thinner soup is desired, add more hot water. Simmer and stir for 15 minutes. Serves 6.

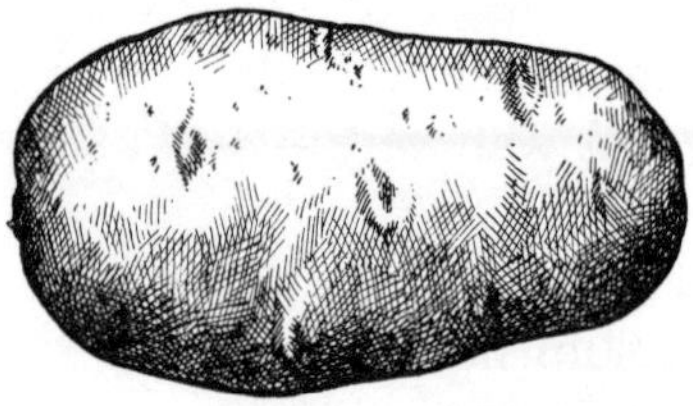

CREAM OF POTATO SOUP

3 medium russet potatoes
1½ tsps salt
white pepper to taste
3 Tbsps butter or margarine
5 cups milk, scalded
¼ cup finely minced green onion

Peel and quarter potatoes, rinse and place in a 4-quart pot. Cover with hot water and boil until very tender. Drain well.

Add salt, pepper and butter to potatoes. Mash well with a potato masher. Add scalded milk. Cook and stir over medium heat for 5 minutes.

Ladle into soup bowls. Sprinkle chopped onions into each bowl. Serves 6.

CREAMY CARROT SOUP

1 lb fresh carrots
1 tsp salt
¼ tsp white pepper
3 Tbsps butter
1 tsp sugar
2 cups milk
⅓ cup flour mixed with ⅔ cup milk
2 cups half-and-half

Peel carrots. Cut into chunks and cover with water in a pot. Boil until very tender. Drain off liquid, saving ¾ cup. Pour saved liquid back in the pot with carrots. Add salt, pepper, butter and sugar.

Mash carrots to a pulp with a potato masher. Add 2 cups milk. Place pot over medium heat until boiling begins. Pour the well-mixed flour mixture slowly into pot, stirring vigorously. Cook, stirring until thickened.

Add half-and-half slowly, stirring as you pour. Heat thoroughly. Serves 6.

SQUASH SOUP

1½ lbs summer squash (crookneck or pattypan)
¼ lb salt pork
water as directed
½ cup chopped onion
2 Tbsps dried vegetable flakes
1½ cups small noodles, broken into 1-inch pieces
½ tsp Italian seasoning
1 tsp salt
⅛ tsp pepper
2 cups chicken or beef broth

Scrub squash and snip off stem and blossom ends. Cut squash into 1-inch cubes and place in a large pot or Dutch oven.

Wash salt pork thoroughly and dry. Cut into cubes. Heat small skillet and add pork cubes. Cook and stir over low heat until most of the fat has cooked out. Add ½ cup of hot water. Stir well and simmer for 1 or 2 minutes.

Add boiling water to cover squash by 3 inches. Pour fat mixture into pot. Add chopped onion and vegetable flakes. Bring to a rolling boil over high heat. Cover with lid, lower heat and simmer for 30 minutes. Add all other ingredients plus 1½ cups boiling water. Turn heat to high and bring to full boil again. Lower heat and simmer for 30 minutes. Serves 6.

CORN CHOWDER

2 medium potatoes
5 Tbsps butter or margarine
5 Tbsps flour
1½ tsps salt
¼ tsp white pepper
4 cups milk
2 Tbsps snipped chives
One 16-oz can cream-style corn (Country Gentleman variety)

Peel potatoes, rinse and cut into ½-inch cubes. Barely cover with lightly salted water. Cook over medium heat until done and drain immediately. Turn potatoes into a soup pot and set aside uncovered.

Melt butter in a large saucepan. Add flour, salt and pepper. Cook and stir over medium heat until smooth. Add 2½ cups of the milk a little at a time, stirring vigorously. Cook and stir until thick. Remove from heat, stir in remaining 1½ cups milk, mixing well.

Pour milk mixture into pot with potatoes. Add chives and corn and stir thoroughly. Place over medium heat. Cook and stir until boiling begins. Remove from heat. Ladle into soup bowls and pass Saltines. Serves 6.

CREAM OF SPINACH SOUP

Two 10-oz packages frozen chopped spinach
water as directed
4 Tbsps butter
1 tsp salt
⅛ tsp lemon pepper
4 cups milk, scalded
⅓ cup flour

Defrost spinach. Place in a pot with 2 cups boiling water. Separate spinach with a fork. Bring to full boil over high heat. Reduce to medium. Cover and cook for 20 minutes.

Remove ¾ cup of the spinach and set aside. Purée remaining spinach in blender. Place all of the spinach back in the pot. Add butter, salt, pepper and scalded milk. Place over medium heat.

When soup is very hot, mix flour with ⅔ cup of cold water. Beat with a fork until all lumps are dissolved. Stirring constantly, pour flour mixture into soup. Cook and stir until thickened. Serves 6.

CABBAGE SOUP

4 cups water
¼ cup minced onion
3 Tbsps dried mixed vegetable flakes
¼ tsp celery seed
3 chicken or beef bouillon cubes
½ tsp salt
½ tsp lemon pepper
4 Tbsps butter or margarine
1 medium head green cabbage, shredded
1½ cups coarsely grated cooked carrots
cheese croutons

Combine 2 cups of the water, minced onion, vegetable flakes, celery seed, bouillon cubes, salt and pepper in a pot. Bring to a boil over medium heat. Stir until bouillon cubes have dissolved.

Melt 2 tablespoons of the butter in a large skillet. Add half the shredded cabbage. Stir and cook until wilted down. Place in the pot. Melt the remaining 2 tablespoons butter in the skillet and cook remaining cabbage.

Add cabbage and remaining 2 cups water to the pot. Bring to a boil, turn heat to low and cover with lid. Simmer slowly for 25 minutes. Add grated carrots and simmer for 15–20 minutes. Float croutons on top of each portion. Serves 4 to 6.

NAVY BEAN SOUP

1 lb dried navy beans
1 1- to 1½-lb meaty soup bone, cracked
1 clove garlic, finely minced
1 cup chopped celery
3 carrots, peeled and sliced
¼ tsp onion powder
½ tsp lemon pepper
1½ tsps seasoned salt
water as directed

Pick through beans and remove any bad ones. Wash beans well, rinse in a colander and let drain. Wash soup bone and place in a 5- or 6-quart pot or Dutch oven. Cover with water and bring to a boil over high heat. Turn burner to low and simmer for 15 minutes. Skim off and discard any scum.

Add beans and all other ingredients except seasoned salt. Bring mixture to a full boil over high heat. Cover with lid, turn burner to low. Simmer slowly, adding boiling water when liquid is needed to keep ingredients covered completely.

Simmer until beans are slightly mushy, liquid is thickened and meat on bone is done. Stir in salt. Add boiling water if a thinner soup is desired. Simmer for a few minutes. Remove from burner and let stand, covered, for 15–20 minutes. Serves 4 to 8.

LIMA BEAN SOUP

2	cups small dried lima beans
	boiling water as directed
1½	cups chopped cooked ham and fat trimmings
2	medium tomatoes, chopped
½	cup chopped green onions
1	bay leaf
½	cup sherry
dash	garlic powder
½	tsp seasoned salt
½	tsp black pepper
½	tsp celery seed
½	tsp rolled sage

Pick through beans and discard any bad ones and foreign matter. Place in colander and rinse well under running water. Transfer beans to a 6-quart pot or Dutch oven.

Add boiling water to cover beans by 3 inches. Place over high heat and bring to a rolling boil. Reduce heat and simmer 30 minutes.

Add prepared ham and trimmings, tomatoes and onions. Place bay leaf on top and pour sherry over beans. Add enough boiling water to measure well above beans. Return to boiling, then reduce heat.

Simmer until beans are tender. Add seasonings and stir well. Continue to simmer, adding water if needed until mixture begins to thicken. Add enough boiling water to make soup the desired consistency. Stir well.

Serve with corn bread. Serves 6.

Note: Near end of cooking time, taste. If salt is needed, add desired amount. Since some ham is very salty, a minimum amount of salt is given in this recipe.

BEEF BARLEY SOUP

3 Tbsps cooking oil
1½ lbs chili-grind (very coarsely ground) beef
½ cup chopped onion
1 clove garlic, minced
water as directed
⅔ cup pearl barley
½ cup chopped celery
4 carrots, peeled and diced
One 10-oz package frozen green peas
1 cup red table wine
¼ cup flour (see directions)
2 tsps salt
½ tsp pepper

Heat oil in a Dutch oven over medium heat. Add meat and separate pieces with fork. Add onion and garlic. Cook and stir until meat is well browned.

Pour 8 cups boiling water over meat, stirring. Add barley and celery. Bring to a boil over high heat. Reduce heat to low and place lid on pot. Simmer for 45 minutes.

Add carrots, peas and wine. Return to boil. Simmer for 30 minutes or until barley and carrots are tender. While soup simmers, brown flour in a small shallow pan in oven to a deep brown (but do not burn). Combine browned flour, salt, pepper and ⅔ cup water. Beat smooth with a fork. Stirring soup constantly, pour in flour mixture. Cook and stir until thickened. If a thinner soup is desired, add boiling water. Serves 6.

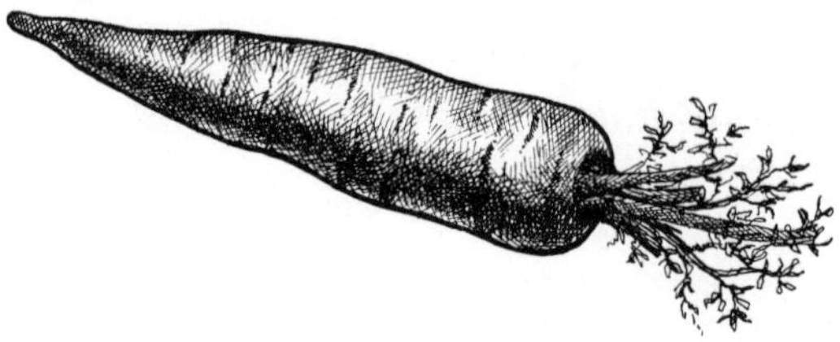

ALBONDIGAS SOUP

1 lb lean ground beef
½ tsp seasoned salt
¼ tsp garlic powder
½ tsp black pepper
water as directed
2 medium tomatoes, cut into thin wedges
1 medium onion, cut into thin wedges
dash cayenne pepper
1 tsp chili powder
1 tsp salt (or more to taste)

With hands, mix ground beef, seasoned salt, garlic powder and pepper, blending well. Shape into meatballs about ¾ inch in diameter. Set aside.

Place tomatoes, onions, cayenne, chili powder and salt in a large pot with 2 cups of water. Bring to a rolling boil over medium heat. Cook for 15 minutes. Add 4 cups of water and bring back to rolling boil.

Drop meatballs one at a time into pot. When boiling resumes, turn heat to low and place lid on pot. Simmer for 30–40 minutes. Serve with toasted tortillas or corn chips. Serves 4 to 6.

CHICKEN GUMBO SOUP

1 small frying chicken
1 lb fresh young okra
1 medium onion, finely chopped
One 16-oz can stewed tomatoes
dash garlic powder
⅛ tsp pepper
1 tsp salt (more to taste)
1½ cups cooked rice
water as directed

Wash chicken. Place in pot and cover with boiling, lightly salted water. Over high heat, bring to a rolling boil. Lower heat and simmer until meat begins pulling from bones.

Transfer chicken to a shallow vessel to cool. Strain broth and allow to cool, then refrigerate until fat has accumulated on top. Skim off and discard most of the fat.

Remove chicken meat from bones, taking care to remove all small bones. Cut into bite-size pieces. Set aside.

Wash okra and remove stem ends. Cut crosswise into ¼-inch-thick slices. Combine okra, onion, tomatoes and seasonings in a saucepan. Add boiling water to cover vegetables by about 1 inch. Cook, uncovered, until vegetables are tender, adding water if necessary and stirring occasionally.

Combine chicken, vegetable mixture and rice in a 5- to 6-quart pot. Add skimmed chicken broth. Bring to a boil over high heat. Lower heat and simmer for 5 minutes. If too thick, add water to desired consistency. Serves 6 to 8.

SALADS

CAULIFLOWER SALAD

1 small head cauliflower
1 small green bell pepper
¼ lb mushrooms, cleaned and sliced
5 red radishes, cleaned and thinly sliced
2 carrots, peeled and thinly sliced
1 small cucumber, peeled and thinly sliced
3 green onions, cleaned and thinly sliced
1 cup oil-and-vinegar dressing
1 tsp salt
½ tsp coarse-ground pepper
dash cayenne pepper
dash garlic powder

Remove core from center of cauliflower. Separate flowerettes and cut into uniform bite-size ones. Rinse well. Place in a bowl of cold salted water. Allow to soak for 30 minutes. Drain well.

Remove and discard seed and core from pepper. Cut pepper into strips. Combine all of the prepared vegetables in a large mixing bowl. Toss well.

Combine dressing, salt, pepper, cayenne and garlic powder. Beat together with a fork. Pour over vegetables and toss. Refrigerate salad and allow to marinate for at least 3 hours, stirring every 30 minutes. Serves 6.

CORN SALAD

4 cups cooked or canned whole-kernel corn, well drained
½ cup chopped celery
¼ cup chopped green onion
¼ cup chopped green bell pepper
¼ cup chopped pimiento or chopped sweet red bell pepper
1 tsp coarse-ground pepper
½ cup Italian dressing (or other of your choice)
3 cups finely shredded lettuce

Combine corn, celery, onion, peppers and ground pepper in a mixing bowl. Toss to blend. Add salad dressing, stirring well. Cover with plastic wrap and refrigerate, stirring occasionally, for 2 hours.

Arrange shredded lettuce in a serving dish or bowl on bottom and up sides. Drain excess dressing from salad and heap corn mixture in center of lettuce bed. Serves 6.

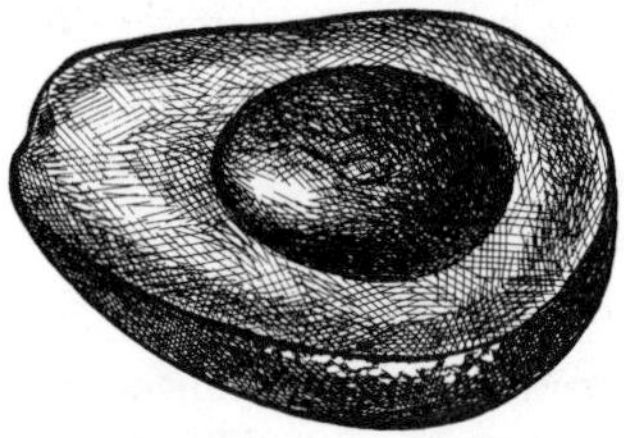

GUACAMOLE SALAD

3 or 4 large ripe avocados
3 Tbsps finely grated onion with juice
1 Tbsp lemon juice
¾ tsp salt
dash garlic powder
dash Tabasco
¼ cup mayonnaise or mayonnaise-type salad dressing
shredded lettuce
ripe olives or tomato wedges

Discard peel and pits of the avocados. Chop meat of avocado finely in a mixing bowl. In a cup, mix all other ingredients together except for the last two. Stir mixture in with avocado, blending well. Heap upon a bed of finely shredded lettuce. Garnish with sliced pitted ripe olives or thin tomato wedges. Serves 6.

COUNTRY BEAN SALAD

- 2 cups cooked or canned cut green beans
- 2 cups cooked or canned pinto beans
- 1 cup cooked or canned green baby lima beans
- 3 small onions, about 1½ inches in diameter
- 6 to 8 red radishes, thinly sliced
- ½ cup thinly sliced celery
- ¾ cup Italian or oil-and-vinegar salad dressing

Combine all of the beans in a colander. Rinse well in cool water and drain thoroughly. Slice onions and pull apart into rings. In a mixing bowl, combine beans, onion rings, prepared radishes and celery. Add salad dressing and toss well. Chill, tossing occasionally to redistribute dressing, for several hours. Before serving, drain off any excess dressing. Serves 4 to 6.

PINEAPPLE CARROT SALAD

- ½ cup white raisins
- 2 cups drained pineapple tidbits or chunks
- 1 lb carrots, peeled and coarsely grated
- ½ pt (1 cup) pineapple yogurt
- 2 Tbsps sugar
- ⅛ tsp salt

Soak raisins in hot water for 30 minutes. Drain, then dry well. Combine raisins, drained pineapple and grated carrots in a mixing bowl.

Mix yogurt, sugar and salt in a small bowl, blending well with a spoon. Add to carrot mixture. Stir and toss until well mixed. Cover and chill until serving time. Serves 4 to 6.

CUCUMBERS AND ONIONS IN SOUR CREAM

2 medium white onions
2 medium cucumbers
½ pt (1 cup) dairy sour cream
2 Tbsps milk
1 tsp salt
½ tsp coarse-ground pepper
paprika
parsley

Peel onions and cucumbers. Slice into rounds. Separate onion slices into rings. Place vegetables in mixing bowl.

Combine sour cream, milk, salt and pepper and mix well. Pour over onions and cucumbers. Toss until vegetables are well coated.

Chill in refrigerator. Sprinkle with paprika and garnish with sprigs of parsley. May be stored for several days in refrigerator. Serves 6 to 8.

TOSSED SPINACH SALAD

1½ lbs fresh young garden spinach
½ cup dairy sour cream
1 Tbsp lemon juice

¼ tsp onion salt
½ tsp salt
dash black pepper
½ tsp sugar
4 slices crisp fried bacon, crumbled
3 hard-cooked eggs, chopped

Wash spinach thoroughly, discarding any discolored leaves and tough stems. Spread spinach out on a large absorbent towel to drain. Chop or tear leaves as for tossed salad.

Combine sour cream, lemon juice, onion salt, salt, pepper and sugar in a large mixing bowl. Mix well. Add spinach. Toss to coat. Add crumbled bacon and chopped eggs. Fold and mix. Refrigerate salad until serving time. Enough for 6.

JULIENNE BEET-APPLE SALAD

Two 16-oz cans julienne beets
2 medium Delicious apples
2 Tbsps milk
⅓ cup mayonnaise
1 Tbsp sugar

Drain beets thoroughly and place in mixing bowl. Peel and core apples and cut into small chunks. Toss beets and apples together.

Mix the milk, mayonnaise and sugar in a cup. Pour over beets and apples. Mix well. Chill until mealtime. Makes a beautiful pink salad. Serves 6.

Note: If you do not find julienne beets in your market, use two 16-oz cans sliced beets. Drain, then cut into narrow strips.

BLACK-EYED PEA SALAD

1-lb package dried black-eyed peas
½ cup chopped celery
⅓ cup chopped green onions
1 cup chopped cooked ham
⅓ cup chopped dill pickle
¼ cup salad dressing of your choice
¼ cup pickle juice

Cook peas as directed on package, only until just done. Do not overcook. Drain in a colander and cool to room temperature.

Combine all ingredients in a large bowl. Mix thoroughly. Serves 6.

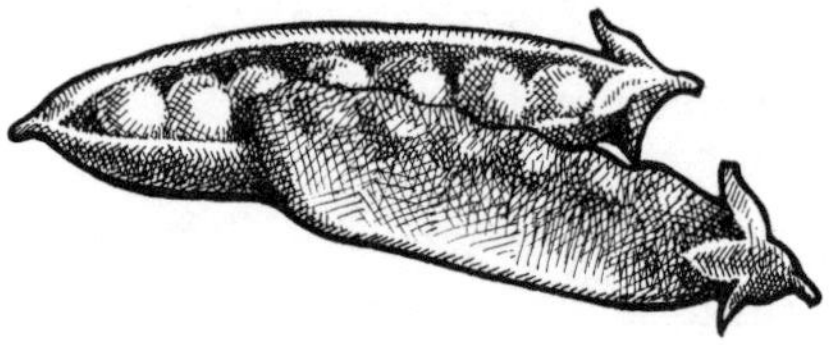

PEA SALAD

Two 16-oz cans green peas, drained
¼ cup sweet pickle relish
¼ cup chopped celery
⅓ cup mayonnaise
½ lb Longhorn cheese, cubed

Combine all ingredients in a mixing bowl. Using two large spoons, toss until mixed thoroughly.

Transfer to serving bowl and refrigerate. Serves 6.

GARDEN SLAW

4 cups coarse-grated cabbage
1 cup coarse-grated carrots
⅓ cup grated green bell pepper
1 cup finely chopped celery
¼ cup finely chopped cucumber
¼ cup finely chopped red radishes
1 cup dairy sour cream
1 Tbsp tarragon vinegar
1 tsp salt
2 tsps sugar
½ tsp coarse-ground black pepper

Combine vegetables in a large mixing bowl. Toss to mix thoroughly. In a small mixing bowl, beat together sour cream, vinegar, salt, sugar and pepper with a fork until smooth and creamy.

Spoon dressing over vegetables and mix until evenly coated. Cover and chill in refrigerator. Garnish with parsley. Serves 4 to 6. Good as a leftover.

MACARONI CHEESE SALAD

One 12-oz package macaroni (shell, twist or elbow)
½ lb Longhorn cheese
¼ cup chopped green onions
¼ cup chopped green bell pepper
¼ cup chopped celery
¼ cup sweet pickle relish
One 3-oz jar pimientos, drained
¾ cup mayonnaise-type salad dressing (or more if desired)

Cook macaroni exactly as directed on package. Drain well. Rinse in cold water and allow to drain completely.

Cut cheese in cubes into a large mixing bowl. Add chopped onions, green pepper and celery, pickle relish, pimientos and salad dressing. Mix thoroughly.

When macaroni is well drained and cool, transfer to mixing bowl with vegetables. Toss until salad is well mixed and macaroni is coated.

Place in serving bowl and cover with plastic wrap. Refrigerate until mealtime. Serves 6 to 8.

OVERNIGHT GREEN SALAD

- 1 medium head iceberg lettuce
- 1 cup coarsely chopped celery
- ½ cup finely sliced red radishes
- ½ cup sliced green onions
- One 10-oz package frozen green peas, defrosted and thoroughly drained
- ½ cup sliced pitted ripe olives
- 1 cup coarsely slivered green bell pepper
- 2 cups mayonnaise
- 2 Tbsps chili sauce
- ½ tsp sugar
- ½ tsp salt
- ⅛ tsp lemon pepper
- ⅛ tsp prepared mustard
- dash cayenne pepper
- 1 cup shredded mozzarella cheese
- ½ cup shredded Swiss cheese
- ripe olives and paprika

Remove and discard outer leaves of lettuce. Pull lettuce apart into bite-size pieces. Place in mixing bowl and salt and pepper lightly. Toss well.

Spread ½ of lettuce on the bottom of a 13x9x2-inch Pyrex dish. Layer with celery, followed by radishes, green onions, peas, olives and bell pepper in that order. Spread remaining lettuce over the bell pepper. Press lightly down with hands.

Combine mayonnaise, chili sauce, sugar, salt, lemon pepper, mustard and cayenne in a mixing bowl. Stir until mixed thoroughly.

Spoon mayonnaise mixture over top of lettuce, spreading it to edge of dish. Sprinkle cheese completely over mayonnaise. Cover and refrigerate for 24 hours before serving. Garnish with ripe olives and sprinkle with paprika. Serves 6.

GREEN VEGETABLE CORN CHIP SALAD

1 head iceberg lettuce
2 large tomatoes, cut into bite-size pieces
¾ cup sliced celery
3 green onions, sliced
6 radishes, sliced
½ cup salad dressing (oil-and-vinegar, or French, etc.)
1 cup Fritos corn chips

Break lettuce into bite-size pieces and crisp for 20 minutes in ice water. Drain well.

Place all of the prepared vegetables in large mixing bowl. Toss until well mixed. Add salad dressing and mix until vegetables are well coated. Just before serving, mix in the Fritos. Serves 6.

MASHED POTATO SALAD

- 4 or 5 large russet potatoes
- ¼ cup sweet pickle relish
- ⅔ cup mayonnaise
- 1 Tbsp prepared yellow mustard
- ⅓ cup milk
- 1 tsp salt (or more to taste)
- ½ tsp coarse-ground pepper
- ½ tsp paprika
- ½ cup chopped celery
- ¼ cup finely sliced green onion
- 2 hard-cooked eggs (for garnish)

Peel and quarter potatoes. Cover with water and boil until well done. As potatoes cook, prepare and measure other ingredients.

Mix pickle relish, mayonnaise, mustard, milk, salt, pepper and paprika together with a fork until smooth and creamy.

When potatoes have cooked, drain and mash thoroughly with a potato masher. Stir in mayonnaise mixture, blending well. Add celery and green onion. Stir until well mixed. Garnish with slices of hard-cooked egg. Serves 6.

CHUNKY POTATO SALAD

- 2 lbs medium-size red potatoes
- ½ tsp coarse-ground pepper
- 1½ tsps salt
- ¾ cup mayonnaise
- ¼ cup milk
- 2 Tbsps prepared mustard
- ¼ cup sweet pickle relish
- ⅓ cup chopped green onion

¼ cup chopped green bell pepper
¼ cup sliced ripe pitted olives
¼ cup chopped celery
3 hard-cooked eggs, coarsely chopped
paprika

Scrub potatoes and boil in jackets until barely done. Drain and allow to cool, then refrigerate for 2 or 3 hours.

Peel potatoes and cut into ½-inch cubes into a large mixing bowl.

Combine pepper, salt, mayonnaise, milk and mustard in a small bowl. Beat until mixed. Add pickle relish and stir. Pour mixture over potatoes.

Add green onion, green pepper, olives, celery and chopped eggs. Blend thoroughly with two large spoons. If mixture seems somewhat dry, more milk may be added. Sprinkle with paprika. Chill in refrigerator. Serves 6.

COTTAGE POTATO SALAD

2 cups cottage cheese
2 Tbsps sugar
¼ cup cider vinegar
1 Tbsp prepared mustard
1 tsp salt (or more to taste)
¼ cup finely chopped onion
¼ cup finely chopped dill pickle
½ cup finely chopped celery
4 cups cubed cooked potatoes
3 hard-cooked eggs, finely chopped

Combine cottage cheese, sugar, vinegar, mustard, salt, onion, pickle and celery in a bowl. Mix well. Add potatoes and eggs. Toss all ingredients until mixed evenly. Cover and chill in refrigerator. Serves 4 to 6.

HAM SALAD

3 cups finely minced cooked ham
1 cup chopped celery
¼ cup chopped green onion
¼ cup chopped parsley
¼ cup chopped green bell pepper
½ cup sliced pitted ripe olives
3 hard-cooked eggs, cut into chunks
½ cup mayonnaise-type salad dressing
2 tsps lemon juice
3 Tbsps milk
1 tsp prepared mustard
shredded lettuce

Combine ham, celery, green onions, parsley, green pepper, olives and eggs in a mixing bowl. Toss until ingredients are distributed evenly.

In a cup, mix salad dressing, lemon juice, milk and mustard by beating with a fork until creamy. Combine dressing with ham mixture in bowl. Stir until dressing coats all ingredients.

Chill until serving time. Arrange bed of shredded lettuce in a serving dish or on individual salad plates and spoon ham salad over lettuce. Serves 6.

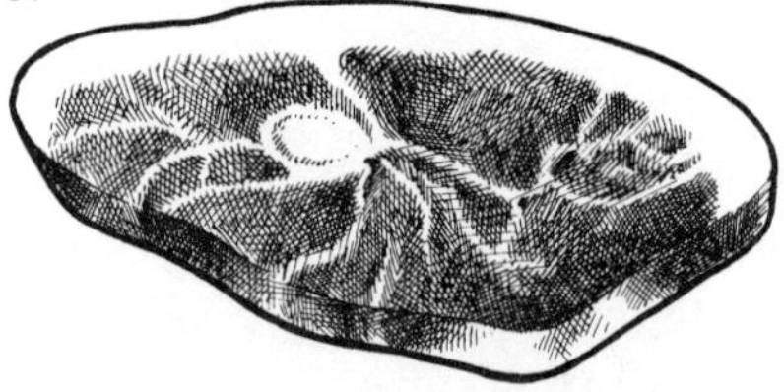

HAM, CHICKEN AND RICE SALAD

4 cups cooked rice (measured after cooking)
1 cup cooked chicken (or turkey) meat, cut into julienne strips
1 cup cooked ham (or canned lunch meat), cut into julienne strips

½ cup sliced pitted large ripe olives
½ cup thinly sliced sweet baby gherkins
½ cup thinly sliced celery
¾ cup Thousand Island or French salad dressing (or more if preferred)
lettuce leaves or shredded lettuce
tomato wedges for garnish
parsley sprigs for garnish

Prepare rice as package directs. Set aside, covered, and allow to cool completely.

Toss together prepared meats, olives, gherkins and celery in a mixing bowl. Fluff rice with a fork and mix it thoroughly with salad dressing. Transfer rice to the mixing bowl and toss all ingredients together until well blended.

Chill. Serve over lettuce leaves or beds of shredded lettuce. Garnish with wedges of tomato and parsley sprigs. Serves 6.

CHICKEN SALAD

4 cups finely diced cooked chicken
1 cup chopped celery
¼ cup chopped green onion
¼ cup sweet pickle relish
½ cup sliced pitted ripe olives
½ cup mayonnaise (or more if desired)
dash cayenne pepper
½ tsp salt
⅛ tsp lemon pepper
3 hard-cooked eggs, sliced

Combine chicken, celery, onion, relish and olives in a mixing bowl. Toss together. In a cup, mix mayonnaise, cayenne, salt and pepper. Add to chicken. Toss until mayonnaise is well distributed. Garnish with egg slices. Serves 6.

Note: Cooked turkey or cooked rabbit may be substituted for the chicken.

FRUITED CHICKEN SALAD

1 large Delicious apple
3 cups cooked chicken, cut into chunks
1 can mandarin orange segments, drained (save juice)
1 cup canned pineapple chunks or tidbits, drained (save juice)
3 large ribs celery, thinly sliced
lettuce or spinach leaves

Dressing:
½ cup mayonnaise, dairy sour cream or plain yogurt
2 Tbsps juice from orange segments
2 Tbsps juice from pineapple
2 Tbsps sugar
1 cup heavy cream, whipped
½ cup coarsely chopped pecans or walnuts

Peel and core apple and chop apple meat. Place in a mixing bowl. Add chicken chunks, orange segments, pineapple and celery. Toss carefully, mixing well, and chill.

To make dressing, mix sugar and juices and stir into mayonnaise. Fold whipped cream and mayonnaise mixture together, blending well.

Place salad on lettuce or spinach leaves. Spoon dressing over salad and top with nuts. Serves 4 to 6.

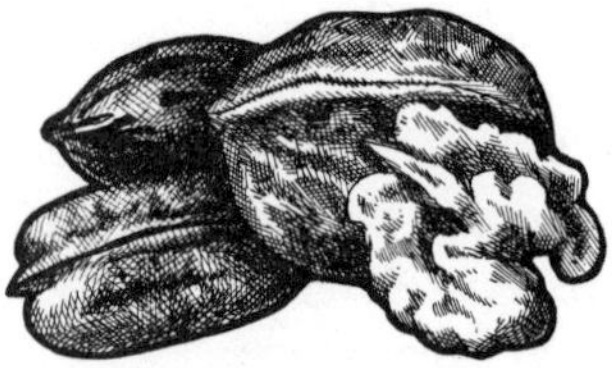

TUNA SALAD

Two 6½-oz cans tuna
½ cup mayonnaise (or more if desired)
2 cups chopped Delicious apples
1 cup chopped celery
½ cup chopped walnuts or pecans
½ cup sliced pitted ripe olives
shredded lettuce

Drain tuna. Place in mixing bowl and flake with a fork. Add mayonnaise and mix thoroughly. Add all other ingredients. Toss together with two spoons until blended evenly.

Make a bed of shredded lettuce in a serving bowl or on individual salad plates. Spoon salad over lettuce. Serves 6.

AVOCADO TOMATO ASPIC

2½ cups tomato juice
2 Tbsps lemon juice
2 Tbsps sugar
½ tsp salt
1 Tbsp sweet pickle relish
2 Tbsps unflavored gelatin
½ cup cold water
3 Tbsps dairy sour cream
3 medium-size ripe avocados (follow directions carefully)
mayonnaise or dairy sour cream

In a pint jar, mix 1½ cups of the tomato juice, lemon juice, sugar, salt and relish. Place the mixture and avocados (unpeeled) separately in refrigerator to chill.

Mix cold water and gelatin in a cup and allow to soften for 5 or

10 minutes. Heat the remaining cup of tomato juice in a saucepan to boiling. Remove from heat and add softened gelatin. Stir until completely dissolved.

Pour mixture into a mixing bowl. Stir in sour cream. Add chilled tomato juice, combining well. Place in refrigerator until mixture has thickened slightly.

Peel and pit chilled avocados. Chop meat of avocados coarsely and stir immediately into tomato mixture to avoid darkening. Turn into a 6-cup mold or individual molds, and chill until firm. Serve on lettuce leaves or beds of shredded lettuce. Top with mayonnaise or sour cream. Serves 6.

TOMATO VEGETABLE ASPIC

1 cup finely shredded cabbage
½ cup minced celery
¼ cup finely shredded carrots
1 Tbsp snipped chives
2 Tbsps lemon juice
2 tsps sugar
½ tsp salt
2½ cups tomato juice
2 Tbsps unflavored gelatin
½ cup cold water
One 3-oz package chilled cream cheese, finely crumbled
lettuce
mayonnaise or dairy sour cream

Toss cabbage, celery and carrots together with the chives and chill.

Stir lemon juice, sugar and salt into 1½ cups of the tomato juice and chill. Mix gelatin and cold water in a cup and let stand for 5 or 10 minutes to soften. Heat the remaining cup of tomato juice to boiling. Remove from heat. Add softened gelatin. Stir until completely dissolved.

Pour gelatin mixture into a large mixing bowl. Stir in the chilled tomato juice mixture. Refrigerate until thickened slightly. Add chilled vegetables and cream cheese and mix well.

Turn into a 6-cup mold or individual molds. Chill until set firm. Serve over lettuce leaves or beds of shredded lettuce. Top with mayonnaise or sour cream. Serves 6.

JELLIED STUFFED TOMATOES

6 ripe but firm tomatoes, 3½ inches in diameter (allow 1 per person)
1¼ cups chicken or beef broth
1 Tbsp lemon juice
1 Tbsp unflavored gelatin softened in 2 Tbsps water
¼ cup finely chopped celery
¼ cup finely chopped cucumber
1 cup cream-style cottage cheese
lettuce
salad dressing

Wash tomatoes and cut off ¼ of the stem part and discard. Scoop out centers and seed. Turn tomatoes cut side down on a plate covered with paper towels. Place in refrigerator to chill.

Heat broth and lemon juice to boiling. Remove from heat and add softened gelatin. Stir until dissolved completely. Chill until partially set. Add celery, cucumber and cottage cheese. Mix well.

Arrange tomatoes cut side up in custard cups. Fill tomatoes with gelatin mixture. Refrigerate for several hours until completely set. Serve as a salad on a bed of shredded lettuce with your favorite salad dressing. Makes 6.

Note: If all the filling is not used, place leftover mixture in a shallow dish and chill until firmly set. Cut into cubes and use as garnish for the stuffed tomatoes.

CHEESE MOUSSE

- ½ cup cold water
- 1 Tbsp unflavored gelatin
- 1¼ cups beef or chicken broth
- 2 Tbsps lemon juice
- ¼ tsp salt
- One 12-oz package cream cheese (or four 3-oz packages)
- 2 Tbsps finely chopped parsley
- 2 Tbsps snipped chives
- 4 or 5 medium round red radishes, finely minced
- 1 egg white
- shredded lettuce
- salad dressing

Place ½ cup cold water in a small saucepan. Sprinkle gelatin slowly into water (do not pour it in all in a heap). Allow gelatin to soften. Add ½ cup of the broth. Place pan over low heat. Stir until gelatin has dissolved completely. Set aside.

Combine remaining broth (¾ cup), lemon juice, salt, cream cheese and gelatin mixture in a blender. Run blender until mixture is smooth. Turn into mixing bowl. Add parsley, chives and radishes. Mix well with a spoon. Beat egg white until stiff. Carefully fold into cheese mixture.

Turn into a large mold or individual molds and refrigerate until completely set. Unmold onto shredded lettuce. Top with favorite dressing. Serves 4 to 6.

AVOCADO AND SHRIMP SALAD MOLD

- One 3-oz package lime-flavored gelatin
- 1 cup boiling water
- 2 Tbsps lemon juice

¾ cup dairy sour cream
3 medium avocados
1½ cups coarsely chopped cooked shrimp
¾ cup finely diced celery

Mix gelatin and boiling water. Stir until completely dissolved. Add lemon juice and sour cream, mixing well. Chill until slightly set.

Peel and pit avocados. Cut flesh into ½-inch cubes. Stir into gelatin mixture immediately to prevent darkening. Add shrimp and celery, stirring until ingredients are distributed evenly.

Turn into a large mold. Chill until firmly set, preferably overnight, before unmolding. Serves 4 to 6.

Note: Drained flaked tuna may be substituted for the shrimp.

MOLDED SALMON SALAD

1 Tbsp unflavored gelatin
1¼ cups chicken or beef broth
¼ cup chili sauce
¼ cup Thousand Island dressing
One 15-oz can pink or red salmon, drained and flaked
¼ cup sliced stuffed olives
¼ cup sliced pitted ripe olives
2 hard-cooked eggs, chopped
¼ cup finely chopped celery

Sprinkle gelatin over broth in a saucepan. Let stand for 10 minutes. Stirring constantly, heat mixture to below boiling. Remove from heat. Stir until gelatin is dissolved completely. Cool for 15 minutes. Add chili sauce and salad dressing. Mix well. Chill mixture until slightly thickened.

While mixture is chilling, place flaked salmon in a large mixing bowl. Add olives, eggs and celery. Add thickened dressing and mix well with a spoon.

Turn into a 4-cup mold and chill until firmly set. This is best chilled overnight before turning out of mold. Serves 4 to 6.

Note: Tuna may be substituted for salmon.

EGGS

DEVILED EGG AND HAM CASSEROLE

4	cups toasted bread cubes
3	cups chopped cooked ham
6	hard-cooked eggs, chopped
1½	tsps prepared horseradish
1½	tsps prepared yellow mustard
2½	cups milk
4	raw eggs
½	tsp salt
¼	tsp pepper

Butter inside of a 13x9x2-inch Pyrex baking dish. Spread 2 cups of bread cubes over bottom of dish. Mix ham, chopped hard-cooked eggs, horseradish and mustard. Spoon over bread cubes in dish. Scatter remaining bread cubes over ham mixture.

Beat milk, eggs, salt, and pepper together until well mixed. Pour over bread cubes. Let stand at room temperature to allow bread to absorb liquid.

Bake slowly in oven preheated to 325° for 45–50 minutes. Serves 6.

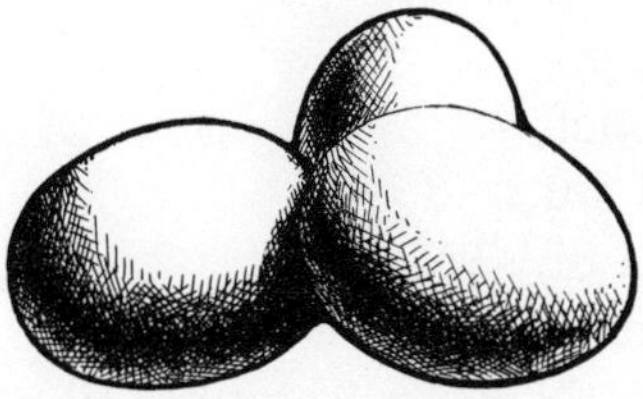

EGGS IN SAUSAGE RING

2 eggs
⅓ cup milk
1 lb bulk uncooked pork sausage
2½ cups bread crumbs
2 Tbsps finely minced onion
scrambled eggs for 6

Preheat oven to 350°. Have ready a 9-inch metal ring mold. In a mixing bowl, beat eggs and milk together until well blended. Add sausage, crumbs, and onion. With hands, mix all together; work like a meat loaf until well blended. Pack the mixture into the ring mold, tamping down with hands firmly.

Place in preheated oven. After 20 minutes, remove from oven and carefully drain off accumulated fat. Return to oven and bake another 20 minutes. Drain off fat again. Turn sausage ring onto a platter and fill with scrambled eggs heaped into center of ring. Serves 6.

Note: Sausage ring may be made ahead, then reheated just before serving.

BEEF SCRAMBLED EGGS

8 eggs, beaten
1 Tbsp cream
½ tsp salt, or more to taste
⅛ tsp white pepper
dash cayenne pepper
1 tsp prepared mustard
2 Tbsps peanut oil
2 cups finely minced cooked roast beef
4 green onions, thinly sliced (optional)
One 2-oz can sliced mushrooms, drained

Combine eggs, cream, salt, pepper, cayenne and prepared mustard in a mixing bowl. Beat until well mixed and frothy.

Heat oil in a large heavy skillet. Add meat and onions. Stir-fry until onions are limp and meat is lightly browned. Add mushrooms. Cook until hot. Pour egg mixture into skillet. Cook and stir to desired consistency. Turn onto a hot platter. Serves 6.

Note: Roast veal, venison, pork, lamb, corned beef, chicken or rabbit may be used as a substitute for the roast beef.

BRAINS 'N' EGGS

2 pairs calves brains
water as directed
1 tsp salt
1 Tbsp vinegar
12 eggs, well beaten
¼ cup heavy cream
⅛ tsp white pepper
¾ tsp salt
4 Tbsps butter, margarine or meat drippings
minced parsley

Cover brains with cold water and leave to soak for 3 hours. Remove any membranes and discolored areas. Cover with water and add 1 tsp salt and 1 Tbsp vinegar. Simmer for 20 minutes. Drain and cover with cold water. When cool, dice the brains into small pieces.

Combine eggs, cream, pepper and salt. Mix well. Melt butter in a large heavy skillet over medium heat. When bubbly, add brains. Stir and cook for 2 or 3 minutes. Add egg mixture. Cook and stir until set to desired doneness. Turn out onto a hot platter. Garnish with minced parsley. Serves 6.

Note: Pork or beef brains may be substituted.

SAUSAGE AND EGG CASSEROLE

- 6 hard-cooked eggs
- 5 Tbsps melted butter or margarine
- ⅓ cup flour, sifted after measuring
- 2¾ cups milk
- ¾ tsp salt
- ⅛ tsp lemon pepper
- 3 slices American cheese, cut into small pieces
- 1 lb pork sausage—cooked, drained and cut into cubes
- Two 12-oz cans mexicorn, drained
- 1 cup bread crumbs

Slice eggs and set aside. Blend melted butter and flour with a spoon in a saucepan over medium heat. Add milk, salt and pepper. Cook and stir constantly until mixture has thickened and is smooth. Add cheese and stir well until melted.

Toss sausage and corn together. Spread ½ of corn and sausage mixture in the bottom of a 2½-quart casserole. Arrange ½ of egg slices on top. Spread remaining corn and sausage over egg slices. Arrange remaining egg slices on top.

Pour sauce over all. Sprinkle with bread crumbs. Bake in oven preheated to 375° for 25–35 minutes. Serves 6.

MEXI EGG BAKE

- 8 eggs
- ¼ cup milk
- 3 Tbsps catsup
- One 10-ounce can chili con carne (without beans)
- 3 Tbsps finely minced onion
- 3 Tbsps finely minced green bell pepper
- One 12-ounce can whole-kernel corn, drained

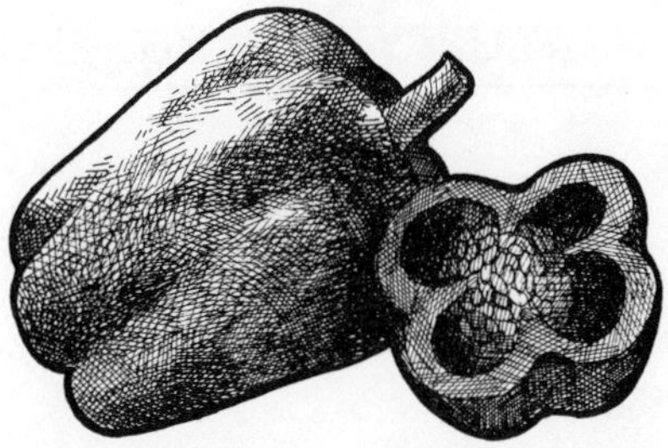

Preheat oven to 350°.

In a large mixing bowl, blend eggs, milk and catsup at medium speed with an electric mixer for 3 or 4 minutes. Remove mixer. With a spoon, combine chili, onion, pepper and corn with eggs, mixing well.

Turn mixture into a large, oblong Pyrex baking dish. Place in the preheated oven until eggs are set like custard (20–25 minutes). Serve at once. Makes 6 to 8 portions.

Great with a green salad and garlic toast.

SCRAMBLED EGGS WITH CORN CHIPS

- 3 Tbsps butter or margarine
- 12 eggs
- 3 Tbsps milk
- 4 Tbsps catsup
- ¾ cup crumbled corn chips

Place the butter in a large heavy skillet over low heat. While butter melts, break the eggs into a mixing bowl. Add milk and catsup to eggs. Beat with an electric mixer at medium speed until frothy.

Pour mixture into the skillet. Cook and stir occasionally until the eggs begin to thicken. Stir in the corn chips, and keep stirring until the eggs are set to desired consistency. Do not overcook. Serves 6.

FLUFFY OMELET

8 egg yolks
⅔ cup cream
1 Tbsp snipped chives (optional)
½ tsp white pepper
1 tsp salt
⅛ tsp celery salt
dash cayenne pepper
8 egg whites
4 Tbsps melted butter
paprika

Preheat oven to 375°. Combine egg yolks, cream, chives and seasonings in a mixing bowl. Beat until well mixed.

In a very large mixing bowl, beat egg whites until peaks will hold shape. Carefully fold yolk mixture into beaten whites. Do not beat.

Heat a very large well-seasoned iron skillet to very hot over medium heat. Pour in melted butter, tilting skillet to coat bottom and sides. Turn egg mixture into skillet. Cook over medium heat (do not stir) until bottom is set. Sprinkle top with paprika.

Place skillet carefully in preheated oven. Bake until set and browned lightly on top. Serves 4 to 6.

TEXAS SCRAMBLE

12 large eggs
1 tsp salt
⅛ tsp white pepper
dash cayenne pepper
3 Tbsps cream
2 large ripe tomatoes

1 Tbsp bacon drippings
4 Tbsps corn oil
¼ cup chopped onion
¼ cup chopped green bell pepper
½ cup shredded Cheddar or American cheese
chili powder
parsley

Combine eggs, salt, pepper, cayenne and cream in a large mixing bowl. Beat with hand mixer until frothy. Set aside. Plunge tomatoes into a pot of boiling water for 2 seconds. Remove immediately and peel. Remove and discard seeds from tomatoes. Cut tomatoes into bite-size pieces. Drain off and discard excess juice.

Pour bacon fat and oil into a large iron skillet. Heat until hot but not smoking. Add onions and green pepper. Stir-fry until vegetables are limp. Add drained tomatoes. Cook only until hot.

Add egg mixture. Cook and stir until eggs are set to desired consistency. Turn onto a large hot platter. Sprinkle shredded cheese and chili powder over top. Garnish with sprigs of parsley or chopped parsley. Serve at once with large hot buttered biscuits. Serves 6.

RANCHERO EGGS

Two 15- or 16-oz cans stewed tomatoes with peppers and onions
One 10-oz can tomatoes with chili peppers
½ tsp salt
1 tsp chili powder
1 tsp parsley flakes (optional)
8 eggs

Mix all ingredients except eggs together in a large skillet. Bring mixture to a full boil over medium heat. Turn burner to low, cover and simmer until cooked down and only about ⅓ of the liquid remains. Leave skillet over burner on low.

Crack eggs one at a time and slide gently onto tomato mixture, spacing eggs in skillet. Salt and pepper tops of eggs lightly. Cover with lid and allow eggs to poach until cooked to desired doneness. Serve on tortillas, corn chips or thick toast. Serves 4 to 8.

CHILI SCRAMBLE

- 12 large eggs
- 3 Tbsps cream
- ⅓ lb brick chili con carne (see note)
- 2 Tbsps cooking oil
- 1 cup slightly crushed corn chips
- ¼ cup chopped onion

Combine eggs and cream in a mixing bowl. Whip until frothy.

With a knife, trim off concentrated tallow (fat) from top of chili and discard. Cut chili into small cubes. Stir into eggs.

Heat oil in a large skillet over medium heat. When hot, add egg mixture. Cook and stir constantly until mixture is set to desired consistency.

Spread corn chips out on a hot platter. Spoon eggs over corn chips. Sprinkle onion over top. Serve at once. Serves 6.

Note: Brick chili comes in 1-lb blocks and may be found in the refrigerated meat department of supermarkets.

DEVILED EGGS

6 hard-cooked eggs, shelled and cut lengthwise
1 small can deviled ham
1 Tbsp prepared mustard
2 Tbsps salad dressing
2 Tbsps snipped chives
½ tsp celery seed
½ tsp salt
dash cayenne pepper
parsley

Remove yolks from whites and place yolks in a mixing bowl. Mash thoroughly with a fork.

Add all other ingredients. Mix well. Stuff into whites with a teaspoon. Round off tops. Garnish with parsley sprigs. Makes 12.

STUFFED EGGS

6 hard-cooked eggs, shelled and cut lengthwise
3 Tbsps mayonnaise
2 tsps prepared mustard
2 Tbsps finely minced green onion
2 Tbsps sweet pickle relish
½ tsp salt
⅛ tsp lemon pepper
paprika

Remove yolks from whites and place yolks in a mixing bowl. Mash well with a fork.

Add all other ingredients. Mix thoroughly. Spoon into whites and round off tops. Sprinkle lightly with paprika. Makes 12.

PICKLED EGGS

- 8 hard-cooked eggs
- 1¼ cups white vinegar
- 1 cup water
- ¼ cup sugar

Peel eggs. Cool eggs and place in a quart jar. Combine vinegar, water and sugar in a saucepan over medium heat. Cook and stir until the mixture is very hot and sugar has melted. Pour over eggs.

After cooling, screw lid on jar and refrigerate. It takes about 2 days for the eggs to pickle. A few drops of food coloring may be added to vinegar mixture if colored eggs are preferred.

Pickled eggs keep well for several days when refrigerated. Use sliced as a garnish or in salad; also good for picnics, buffets, and for snacks.

MEATS

ROAST BEEF

	5- to 6-lb rolled rump roast
3 or 4	cloves garlic
	seasoned salt
	lemon pepper
1	can flat beer

Cut each clove of garlic into 6 pieces lengthwise. With a very slender knife, puncture meat and insert a sliver of garlic. Continue inserting the garlic, spreading it over meat until all slivers are used.

Rub salt and pepper over entire surface of meat. Make a loose tent of foil and lay over top and sides of meat. Do not press down. Place on rack in roasting pan in oven preheated to 450°. Cook for 20 minutes, then lower heat to 325°. Baste meat with beer. From this point, cook 30 minutes per pound of meat—2½ hours for 5 pounds, 3 hours for 6 pounds. Lift tent and baste occasionally with beer and drippings in roaster. Serves 6, with leftovers.

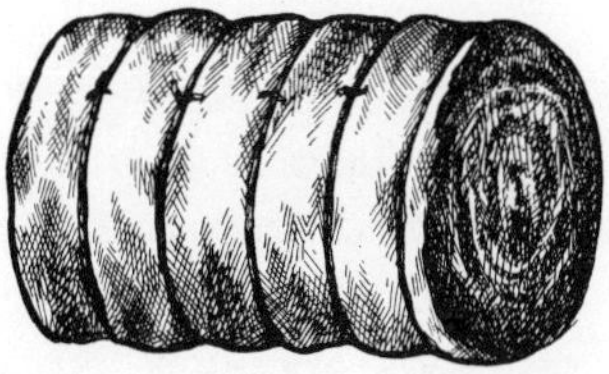

TEXAS POT ROAST WITH BROWN GRAVY

4- to 5-lb beef round pot roast
3 cloves garlic
2 tsps seasoned salt
pepper
parsley
12 onions, 2½ inches in diameter, peeled
6 ribs celery
12 large carrots, peeled
12 red potatoes, about 3 inches in diameter, peeled
5 Tbsps flour mixed with ¾ cup water

Trim excess fat from roast. Cut each clove of garlic into 6 slivers. With a very narrow knife, puncture meat to a depth of 1½ inches. Stuff a sliver of garlic into each slit, all the way down, with finger. Stuff a small sprig of parsley after the garlic. Use ½ of garlic slivers on each side of meat, spreading out the punctures over meat evenly.

Sprinkle ½ of salt and some pepper over top of roast. Rub in with hands. Turn roast and rub in remaining salt and more pepper. Pour 3 tablespoons of oil into a large electric skillet or very large iron skillet. Heat oil to sizzling. Transfer roast to skillet and brown each side thoroughly.

If using electric skillet, pour 3 cups of water around roast. Bring to full boil, turn to simmer. Place lid tightly on meat. If not using electric skillet, transfer meat to a large kettle containing 3 cups of water. Bring to rolling boil, reduce heat to simmering. Place lid on kettle.

Add boiling water occasionally when needed and run a spatula under meat to keep it from sticking to pot. Cook for 30 minutes, then place onions and celery on top of meat. Check liquid, then cover tightly. Remove onions and celery when done. Cook meat 2 hours, then arrange potatoes and carrots over or around meat. When vegetables are tender, remove from pot.

Meat should be cooked in 3–4 hours depending on tenderness of the piece. Check with a fork. During last few minutes of cooking, return vegetables to pot and heat. Transfer meat and vegetables to serving dishes and keep hot in a warm oven while making gravy.

Skim fat from liquid in pot. Measure liquid and add water to measure 3 cups. Return to pot over medium heat. Stir flour-water mixture vigorously and pour into pot. Stir constantly until gravy has thickened. Taste for salt. If needed, add to taste and mix well. Serves 6.

BRAISED SHORT RIBS

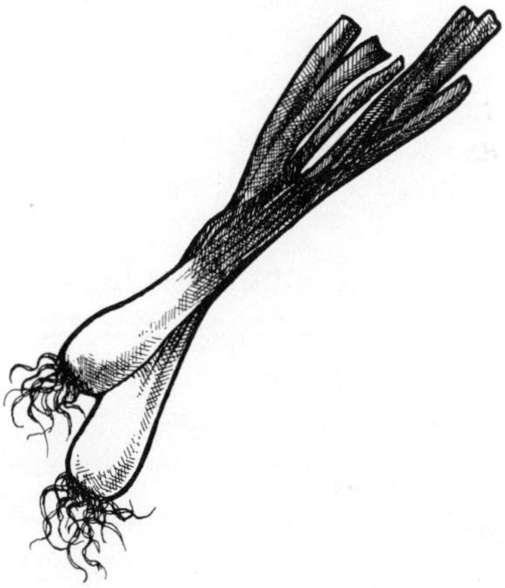

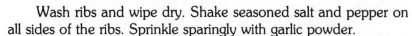

- 4 lbs lean beef short ribs
- seasoned salt
- pepper
- garlic powder
- 2 Tbsps cooking oil
- 1 cup red table wine
- 3 Tbsps soy sauce
- water as directed
- ½ cup chopped green onion
- ½ cup chopped celery
- ½ cup grenadine
- 2 Tbsps vinegar
- 2 Tbsps cornstarch mixed with ¼ cup water

Wash ribs and wipe dry. Shake seasoned salt and pepper on all sides of the ribs. Sprinkle sparingly with garlic powder.

Heat oil in a Dutch oven over medium heat. Brown ribs on all sides. Drain on absorbent paper. When all are browned, pour off and discard all fat from pan. Return meat to Dutch oven.

Mix wine and soy sauce. Pour over meat. Add enough boiling water to cover meat. Place onion and celery over ribs. Bring to a rolling boil over high heat. Cover tightly with lid. Turn heat to low and simmer until meat is tender.

Remove meat from pot. Add grenadine, vinegar and cornstarch mixture to broth in pot. Cook and stir until thickened. Place meat back into the pot and coat with sauce. Simmer for 2 or 3 minutes. Serves 6.

BREADED CUTLETS

6 large veal, beef, pork or venison cutlets
2 eggs
¼ cup dairy sour cream
2 Tbsps milk
¾ tsp salt
⅛ tsp pepper
very fine dry bread crumbs or cracker meal
peanut oil

Pound meat until very thin. Combine eggs, sour cream, milk, salt and pepper in a mixing bowl. Beat until well mixed and frothy. Dip cutlets 1 at a time into egg mixture, then coat well with crumbs or cracker meal.

Spread coated meat side by side on wax paper. Allow to stand, turning once, for about 15 minutes.

Pour oil ¼ inch deep into a heavy skillet. Heat oil until sizzling but not smoking. Cook cutlets quickly on each side until lightly browned.

Serve with Cream Gravy (see page 121) or your favorite sauce. Makes 6 portions.

RAGOUT OF VEAL

2 lbs boneless veal shoulder, cut into 1½-inch cubes
2 Tbsps oil
¼ cup burgundy or port wine
¼ tsp pepper
2 tsps salt
dash cayenne pepper
dash garlic powder
water as directed
1 lb small carrots
8 boiling onions
8 small red potatoes, peeled
8 ribs celery
1 lb fresh green beans

Heat oil in a large heavy skillet. Brown meat on all sides. Add wine, pepper, salt, cayenne, garlic powder and 1 cup of water. Bring mixture to a full boil, reduce heat to low and cover with lid. Simmer slowly for 45 minutes. Add more boiling water when needed.

While meat cooks, peel carrots, leaving them whole, and rinse. Peel onions. Wash green beans thoroughly and remove any strings. Gather whole beans into a bunch and tie in center with a string. Cut each celery rib into two pieces crosswise.

Transfer meat mixture to a Dutch oven. Add vegetables and 1 cup of water. Bring to a rolling boil, then turn heat to low and cover. Simmer until vegetables are tender. If desired, the cooking juices may be thickened. Serves 4 to 6.

TEXAS SWISS STEAK

2 lbs boneless round steak (pounded to tenderize)
salt
pepper
flour for dredging
½ cup cooking oil (or more if needed)
2 large onions
Two 16-oz cans tomatoes
2 cups water
1 clove garlic, finely minced

Cut tenderized steak into serving-size pieces. Salt and pepper lightly both sides of each piece. Dredge in flour to coat each side, shaking off excess.

In a very large iron skillet, Dutch oven or large electric skillet, heat oil to sizzling. Quickly brown each side of steak lightly. Remove meat from oil and blot with paper towels. Drain off and discard oil and return steak to skillet.

Arrange onions on top of meat, add tomatoes, water and garlic. Place over high heat until mixture begins to boil. Turn burner to a slow simmer. Place lid on skillet and allow meat to cook until very tender (about 1 hour). While cooking, stir occasionally and scrape bottom of skillet with spatula to prevent sticking. Serve with rice. Makes 4 to 6 portions.

SMOTHERED STEAK AND MUSHROOMS

6 large cube steaks
flour
salt
lemon pepper
½ cup light cooking oil

½ lb small mushrooms
¼ cup sherry wine
water as directed

Lightly salt and pepper the sides of each steak. Dredge in flour until heavily coated. Place on wax paper on counter.

Heat oil in large iron skillet over high heat until sizzling hot. Shake excess flour from steaks and place meat in hot oil. Brown quickly on both sides and drain on absorbent paper.

Clean mushrooms and cut in halves, if small. Larger ones should be cut into 4 pieces. Place in oil where meat has cooked. Over medium heat, cook until lightly browned. Remove mushrooms from oil and drain on absorbent paper.

Pour off and discard oil in skillet. Place skillet back over medium heat. Pour 2½ cups of boiling water into skillet. Allow to simmer. Stir with spoon, loosening all particles left in skillet. When loosened, remove skillet from burner.

Place steaks side by side in liquid in skillet. Arrange mushrooms around steaks. Pour sherry over steaks.

Cook in oven preheated to 350° for 40–45 minutes. Stir gravy once during cooking. Serves 6.

PEPPER STEAK

1½ lbs boneless steak or roast, cut into thin strips
¼ cup light vegetable oil
1 cup water
¼ cup soy sauce
½ tsp salt
1 tsp coarse-ground pepper
dash garlic powder
2 green bell peppers, cored, seeded and cut into strips
1 large onion, cut into chunks and separated
1 cup sliced celery
2 Tbsps cornstarch mixed with 1 cup of water
3 small tomatoes, cut into wedges
hot cooked rice

In a large skillet, sauté meat in hot oil until evenly browned. Add water, soy sauce, salt, pepper and garlic powder. Bring to a brisk boil over medium heat. Cover with lid and reduce heat to low. Simmer slowly for 45 minutes or until tender.

Add green pepper, onion and celery. Stir well, cover and let cook slowly for 15 minutes. Add well-mixed cornstarch and water. Cook and stir until thickened slightly and clear. Add tomato wedges and stir well. Bring to a boil. Cover and let cook for 2 or 3 minutes. Serve over rice. Serves 4 to 6.

DEVILED STEAK

- 3 lbs beef round steak, pounded vigorously on both sides
- 4 Tbsps flour
- 2 tsps dry mustard
- 1½ tsps seasoned salt
- ½ tsp lemon pepper
- 3 Tbsps light oil
- ½ cup Sauterne wine
- 1¼ cups hot water
- 1 Tbsp prepared horseradish
- 2 Tbsps snipped chives
- 2 Tbsps chopped parsley

Cut pounded steak into serving-size pieces. Combine flour, dry mustard, salt and pepper. Mix well. Sprinkle evenly ½ of the mixed dry ingredients over one side of the steak pieces. Pound into steak. Turn meat and pound remaining dry ingredients into meat.

In a large heavy skillet, sear steak quickly in hot oil to a golden brown on each side. Mix wine, water and horseradish together. Pour mixture over steak in skillet. Sprinkle chives and parsley over meat.

Bring to a boil over medium heat. Reduce heat to low and cover tightly with lid. Simmer slowly for 60–75 minutes or until steak is tender. Serves 6.

STEAK WITH SEASONED BUTTER

1 lb butter
⅛ tsp white pepper
1 Tbsp finely chopped parsley
2 Tbsps lemon juice
1 Tbsp grated fresh or bottled horseradish
1 tsp sugar
½ tsp dry mustard
1 Tbsp finely grated onion
6 individual steaks of your choice

Soften butter at room temperature for 1 hour. Transfer to a small mixing bowl. Add all other ingredients (except steaks). Cream with the back of a spoon, then beat until mixed thoroughly.

Preheat broiler. Spread seasoned butter over one side of each steak. Place under broiler, butter side up. Cook according to your preference of doneness. Remove from broiler and spread seasoned butter on other side of each steak. Return to broiler until cooked to your liking.

Serve with toast spread with remaining seasoned butter. Leftover butter may be refrigerated for later use. Serves 6.

SALISBURY STEAKS WITH CHILI RAREBIT

1 tsp salt
2 tsps soy sauce
2 Tbsps Worcestershire sauce
⅛ tsp garlic powder
2 lbs lean ground beef
1 medium onion, finely minced
3 Tbsps cooking oil
1 cup water
One 15-oz can chili con carne (without beans)
1½ cups shredded American cheese
⅔ cup flat beer or ale

Combine salt, soy sauce, Worcestershire sauce and garlic powder. Mix well. Place meat and onion in a mixing bowl. Pour sauce mixture over meat. With hands, work and knead until thoroughly blended. Shape into 6 thick patties.

Pour oil into skillet and heat to sizzling. Brown meat lightly on each side. Drain off oil and add water. Bring to a boil, then lower heat. Place lid on skillet and allow patties to simmer until water has been absorbed. Remove from heat.

Combine chili, cheese and beer in a saucepan. Cook and stir constantly over medium heat until cheese has melted and mixture is very hot. Place patties on a hot platter and spoon chili rarebit over tops. Serve with thick toast or toasted buns. Serves 6.

STUFFED STEAK ROLLS

1 medium onion
1 cup chopped celery
4 Tbsps butter
½ cup milk

½ cup shredded Swiss, American or Cheddar cheese
1 cup cracker crumbs
Two 4-oz cans sliced mushrooms
6 cube steaks (1½ to 2 lbs)
salt
pepper
¼ cup light vegetable oil
½ cup red table wine
1 cup water
1 tsp soy sauce

Sauté onion and celery in butter, stirring until light golden brown. Add milk and cheese. Stir until cheese has melted. Remove from heat. Combine with crumbs and mushrooms, mixing well.

Spread wax paper on flat surface and place steaks in a row on paper. Lightly salt and pepper steaks. Divide cheese mixture on center of steaks and spread, but do not spread to the edges. Roll steaks tightly and tie with string.

In an electric skillet, lightly brown steaks on all sides in hot oil. Drain meat on absorbent paper and drain oil thoroughly from skillet. Return steaks to skillet.

Add wine, water and soy sauce. Bring to a boil and lower heat. Cover with lid, simmer slowly, turning steaks occasionally, for 30–40 minutes. Makes 6 portions.

SEASONED CHICKEN-FRIED MOCK STEAK

1¼ lbs lean ground beef, veal, lamb or pork
3 Tbsps finely chopped parsley
1 tsp seasoned salt
1 tsp onion powder
2 tsps steak sauce
1 egg
¼ cup cracker meal
½ cup cooking oil
flour for dredging

Mix ground meat, parsley, salt, onion powder, steak sauce, egg and cracker meal thoroughly with both hands as for meat loaf. Cover and refrigerate for 2 hours.

Divide into 6 equal parts. Shape into patties; or, for a real gourmet touch, shape like pork or lamb chops. Dredge well in flour.

Pour cooking oil into a large skillet. Place over medium heat until oil is sizzling hot. Quickly fry "steaks," browning on both sides. Drain on absorbent paper. Serve with favorite gravy or sauce. Makes 6 portions.

BEEF 'N' SAUSAGE

- 1 lb country pork sausage
- 1½ lbs beef, cut into bite-size cubes
- ½ lb small mushrooms
- 1 clove garlic, minced
- ½ tsp salt
- 4 or 5 green onions, cut into ¼-inch lengths
- water
- 1 cup flat beer

Shape sausage into patties. Cook in a Dutch oven until lightly brown. Drain patties on absorbent paper and set aside. Place beef cubes in the pot, cooking and stirring until evenly browned. Drain grease from meat and discard.

Add mushrooms, garlic, salt and green onions. Cover mixture with water. Bring to a rapid boil, then turn burner to low and cover pot with lid. Simmer until meat is almost tender.

Cut sausage patties into bite-size pieces. Add the sausage and beer to the pot. Stir to distribute ingredients evenly. Bring to a rapid boil once more, cover and turn burner back to low. Simmer slowly until beef is tender. Gravy may be thickened if desired. Good with sourdough bread. Serves 6.

BRAISED OXTAILS

4 lbs oxtails, cut into joints
¾ cup flour
1 tsp salt
¼ tsp pepper
¼ cup peanut oil
3 Tbsps catsup
2 Tbsps A-1 sauce
1 tsp Worcestershire sauce
½ cup red wine
2 cups water
¼ cup finely chopped celery
1 Tbsp cornstarch mixed with ¼ cup water

Wash oxtail joints thoroughly and dry. Combine flour, salt and pepper in a paper bag. Shake joints in mixture to coat. Heat oil in a Dutch oven until hot but not smoking. Brown joints on all sides. Drain on absorbent paper. Drain off and discard oil.

Combine catsup, A-1 sauce, Worcestershire sauce, wine and water in Dutch oven. Bring to a rolling boil. Add oxtail joints. Top with celery. When boiling resumes, cover with lid and turn burner to low. Simmer 2–3 hours or until meat is very tender. Turn meat several times during cooking to steep it well.

When done, lift out joints with a slotted spoon and place on a large heavy platter. Keep hot in warm oven.

Pour well-mixed cornstarch and water into pot, stirring constantly. Cook and stir until thickened. Spoon pot liquid over oxtails. Serves 6.

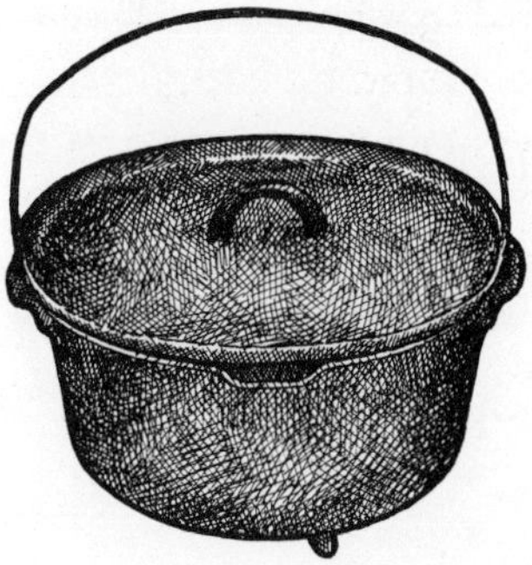

ROAST BEEF HASH

3 Tbsps cooking oil
3 cups finely chopped cooked roast beef
1 large onion, chopped
3 large russet potatoes
One half 4-oz can chopped green chili peppers (optional)
1½ tsps salt
½ tsp pepper
water as directed

Heat oil in a Dutch oven over high heat. Add beef. Cook and stir until meat is browned lightly. Add onions. Stir for 1 minute.

Pour 2 cups water in pot and cover with lid. Turn heat to medium.

Peel potatoes and rinse. Cut into small cubes. Stir chili peppers, salt and pepper into pot with meat. Place potatoes on top and cover.

Stir mixture occasionally and check water level. If too low, add small amount of boiling water. Cook until potatoes are tender and liquid is low. Makes 6 portions.

SCRAPPLE

4 cups water
¼ tsp rubbed sage
1½ tsps salt
½ tsp pepper
3 Tbsps grated onion with juice
1 cup quick grits
2 cups finely minced cooked or lean ground meat or fowl of your choice
flour for dusting
cooking oil

Combine water, sage, salt, pepper and onion in a pot. Bring to a rolling boil over medium heat. Stirring constantly, pour grits slowly into the boiling liquid. When mixture returns to a full boil, reduce heat to low. Simmer 4–5 minutes, stirring occasionally. Remove from heat.

Add prepared meat or fowl and stir well to mix. Pack into a well greased 9x5x3-inch loaf pan. Cover and refrigerate overnight. Turn scrapple from pan. Cut into ½-inch-thick slices. Dust each slice with flour and brown in hot oil. Great for breakfast, brunch or supper. Serves 6.

STUFFED PEPPERS

3	very large green bell peppers
1½	lbs lean ground beef
½	cup catsup
1	Tbsp Worcestershire sauce
dash	garlic powder
1	tsp salt
½	tsp rubbed sage
	pepper to taste
1	medium onion, finely minced
2	ribs celery, finely minced
¼	cup cracker meal

Cut peppers in half through center of core. Remove seeds and stem end. Wash well. Turn cut side down on paper towels and allow to drain.

Combine all other ingredients in a large mixing bowl. Work with hands as for meat loaf. Continue kneading until all ingredients are distributed evenly.

Stuff peppers but do not pack tightly. Round the tops. Place in a baking dish. Pour water about ½ inch deep in pan.

Bake in oven preheated to 350° for 45–50 minutes. Serve with Salsa (see page 195). Makes 6 portions.

SMOKY BARBECUE LOAF

2 eggs
⅓ cup bottled or homemade barbecue sauce
1 tsp liquid smoke
1 Tbsp prepared yellow mustard
½ tsp pepper
1 tsp salt
2 lbs lean ground beef
¼ cup finely minced onion
1 cup fine dry bread crumbs
2 medium carrots, finely grated

Oil lightly bottom of a 9x5x3-inch loaf pan. Combine eggs, barbecue sauce, liquid smoke, mustard, pepper and salt in a small bowl. Beat together until well blended.

Place ground meat in a large mixing bowl. Add egg mixture. With both hands, work until mixed thoroughly. Add onion, crumbs and carrots. Knead with hands until ingredients are distributed evenly.

Pat mixture into loaf pan. Bake in oven preheated to 400° for 20 minutes, then lower heat to 325°. Bake for 1¼ hours before turning out of pan. Makes 1 loaf.

CHILI CON CARNE

2 lbs chili-grind (very coarsely ground) beef
2 Tbsps cooking oil
3 Tbsps minced dried onion
One 16-oz can stewed tomatoes
One 10-oz can tomato soup
¼ cup catsup
2½ cups water
½ tsp garlic powder

1 Tbsp chili powder
½ tsp crushed dried red peppers
Two 1.75-oz packages chili seasoning mix

Heat oil in a Dutch oven. Add meat, separating pieces with a fork. Cook and stir constantly over medium heat. Add onion and cook, stirring until meat is browned.

Add tomatoes, cutting each into small pieces. Stir in soup, catsup and water. Bring to a rolling boil. Add garlic powder, chili powder and crushed peppers. Stir well. Cover with lid and lower heat. Simmer until meat is very tender, about 45 minutes, adding a small amount of hot water if it seems necessary.

Add chili mix, stirring thoroughly. Cover with lid and simmer for 15–20 minutes, stirring occasionally. For a thinner chili, add more hot water. Cooked beans may be added with chili mix.

Serve with Saltines. Makes 6 servings with seconds.

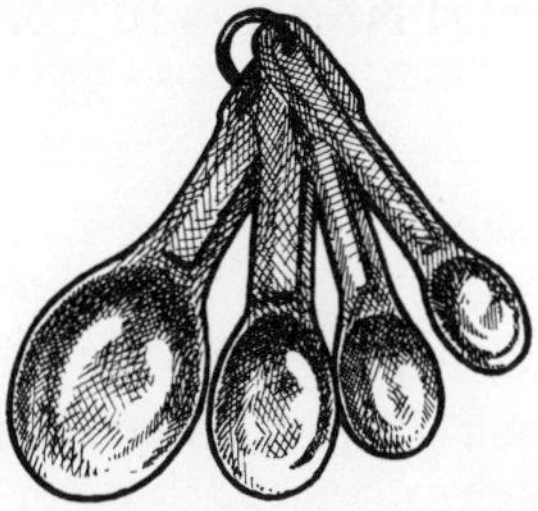

BEANS WITH HERBED MEATBALLS

1 lb dried navy beans (small white beans)
½ cup finely minced green onions and tops
2 Tbsps finely minced parsley
1 egg
1 Tbsp Worcestershire sauce
dash Tabasco
½ tsp celery salt
⅛ tsp ground coriander
⅛ tsp powdered dill
½ tsp lemon pepper
1 lb lean ground beef
½ cup very fine dry bread crumbs

Pick through beans and remove any bad ones. Cook beans as directed on the package. Salt as directed. Add onions and parsley to pot with beans.

While beans are cooking, make meatballs. Beat egg with Worcestershire sauce, Tabasco, celery salt, coriander, dill and pepper. Mix well. Combine egg mixture with meat in a mixing bowl. Work with the hands as for meat loaf. Add bread crumbs and mix thoroughly. Shape into tight balls (any size desired).

When beans are nearly done, place meatballs on top. Make certain that beans contain sufficient water. Bring mixture to a full boil, then reduce heat to low. Cover tightly with lid and simmer until beans are very tender. Serves 4 to 6.

MORE
(Ground Beef and Noodles in Tomato Sauce)

3 Tbsps cooking oil
1 lb lean ground beef
1 medium onion, chopped
1 medium green bell pepper, cored, seeded and chopped
1 cup chopped celery
One 16-oz can stewed tomatoes
One 10-oz can tomato sauce
1½ cups water
¼ cup catsup
1 Tbsp Worcestershire sauce
2 Tbsps dried vegetable flakes
dash Tabasco
dash cayenne pepper
¼ tsp pepper
½ tsp salt
One 12-oz package egg noodles

Heat oil in a Dutch oven. Add beef, onion, green pepper and celery. Separate meat with a fork. Cook and stir over medium heat until meat is lightly browned.

Add tomatoes and cut into smaller pieces. Add tomato sauce, water, catsup, Worcestershire sauce, vegetable flakes and seasonings. Stir well. Bring to a rolling boil over high heat. Cover tightly with lid and reduce heat to low. Cook for 20 minutes.

Remove lid. Boil mixture until it thickens like catsup. Remove from burner and cover with lid.

Cook noodles in lightly salted water as directed on the package. When tender, drain in a colander. Turn noodles into Dutch oven with sauce. Mix well. Heat only until hot. Serve with garlic toast and green salad. Makes 6 portions.

BAKED SPAGHETTI

1-lb package spaghetti
3 Tbsps cooking oil
1 lb lean ground beef
1 cup chopped onion
½ cup finely minced celery
½ cup finely minced green bell pepper
Two 10-oz cans tomato soup
One 12-oz can tomato paste
3 cups boiling water
1 tsp Italian seasonings
⅛ tsp garlic powder
½ cup grated Parmesan cheese

Break spaghetti into 3-inch lengths and cook according to directions on package. Do not overcook. Drain and set aside, covered.

Heat oil in a Dutch oven. Add meat and separate pieces with a fork. Add onion, celery and green pepper. Cook and stir over medium heat until meat is browned lightly.

Add soup, tomato paste, water and seasonings. Stir well. Bring to a rolling boil over high heat. Reduce heat. Simmer, stirring occasionally, 30 minutes.

Combine sauce and spaghetti in pot. Stir thoroughly. Turn into a 13x9x2-inch baking dish. Sprinkle cheese over top. Bake in oven preheated to 400° for 20 minutes or until bubbly. Serves 6.

ENCHILADA CASSEROLE

1 lb lean ground beef
4 cups partially crushed corn chips
1 cup tomato sauce
2 eggs
1 package enchilada sauce mix
1 cup water
1½ cups chili con carne without beans (undiluted)
¼ cup finely minced onion
⅔ cup sliced pitted ripe olives, drained
1 cup (4 ozs) shredded natural Cheddar cheese

Preheat oven to 325°. Brown beef in an iron skillet, breaking into small pieces as it cooks. Brown lightly but thoroughly. Drain off fat.

Spread ½ of the crushed corn chips in the bottom of a baking dish. Spoon meat on top. Blend tomato sauce, eggs, enchilada sauce mix and water on medium speed with a hand mixer. Stir in chili con carne and minced onion, mixing well. Pour evenly over meat.

Sprinkle olives on top, then remainder of crushed corn chips. Bake uncovered for 35–40 minutes. Sprinkle cheese on top and return to oven for 10 minutes. Spoon onto plates. Good with a green salad and garlic toast. Serves 6.

CHEESEBURGER PIE

One 8-oz package corn chips, coarsely crushed
1½ lbs lean ground beef
¾ cup chopped onion
1½ cups water
¼ cup catsup
⅔ tsp salt
One 10-oz can condensed Cheddar cheese soup

Place ⅔ of the crushed corn chips in a large casserole and set aside.

In a large skillet, separate meat with a fork. Add onion. Cook and stir over medium heat until meat is lightly browned, and there is no longer any pink and it is well separated. Drain off any fat.

Add water, catsup and salt. Bring to a boil over medium heat. Cover and turn burner to low. Simmer slowly until liquid has cooked down to about one half. Stir in soup and mix well.

Pour into prepared casserole over corn chips. Sprinkle remaining chips over top. Bake slowly, in oven preheated to 325°, for 30–40 minutes. Serves 4.

CORNED BEEF AND DRESSING BAKE

4 cups crumbled stale white bread
4 cups crumbled corn bread
water as directed
1 cup diced celery
½ cup chopped green onion
One 12-oz can corned beef, chopped
1 tsp poultry seasoning
½ tsp rubbed sage
½ tsp pepper
3 tsps beef or chicken bouillon granules
¼ cup finely chopped parsley

Grease a 13x9x2-inch baking dish. Place crumbled breads in a large mixing bowl and set aside.

Combine 1½ cups water, celery and green onions in a large saucepan. Cook until vegetables are almost tender. Add chopped corned beef, poultry seasoning, sage, pepper, bouillon granules and 2 cups more water, mixing well. Bring mixture to a boil, turn heat to low and simmer for 10–15 minutes.

Stir in parsley. Heat mixture to steaming and pour over crumbled breads. Mix well but carefully with a spoon.

Turn into prepared baking dish and place in oven preheated to 350°. Bake until set and browned lightly on top. Serve Corned Beef and Dressing as an entrée with your favorite gravy. Serves 4 to 6.

BARBECUED CHIPPED ROAST BEEF BURGERS

1 cup homemade or bottled barbecue sauce
¼ cup water
3 cups chopped cooked roast beef
6 medium-size split hamburger buns, heated

Stir barbecue sauce and water together in a saucepan over medium heat. When the sauce begins to boil, cook and stir for 2 or 3 minutes.

Add prepared beef and mix with sauce. Cook and stir until mixture has thickened and beef is hot. Spoon mixture between bun halves. Makes 6.

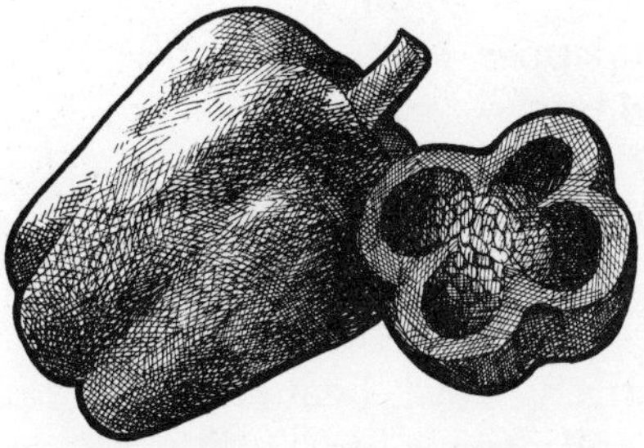

CHUCK WAGON SLOPPY JOES

- 1½ lbs lean ground beef, veal, venison, pork or lamb
- 1 medium onion, chopped
- 1 small green bell pepper, finely chopped
- 1 cup bottled or homemade barbecue sauce
- 1 tsp liquid smoke
- 1 clove garlic, finely minced
- ½ tsp seasoned salt
- ¼ tsp lemon pepper
- 1 cup water
- 6 to 8 hamburger buns

Combine ground meat, onion and green pepper in a Dutch oven over medium heat. Break up meat into very fine bits while cooking and stirring. Continue until meat loses all pink and is lightly brown. Add all other ingredients and mix well with a spoon.

Bring mixture to a boil, cover with a lid and turn burner to low. Simmer until mixture is cooked down to the consistency of thick catsup. Spoon onto hot buns. Makes 6 to 8 burgers.

RANCH BEEF BURGERS

1 egg
1½ tsps prepared mustard
1½ tsps soy sauce
1 tsp Worcestershire sauce
½ tsp salt
¼ tsp lemon pepper
1½ lbs ground beef
¼ cup finely chopped parsley
¼ cup finely chopped green onion
¼ cup fine dry bread crumbs

In a large mixing bowl, beat egg until creamy. Add mustard, the sauces, salt and pepper. Beat well.

Add meat and work with hands until well blended. Add parsley, green onion and crumbs. Mix until all ingredients are distributed evenly. Shape into 6 patties. Grill, broil or pan-fry to desired doneness. Makes 6.

RANCH LAMB BURGERS

Use recipe for Ranch Beef Burgers except substitute 1½ lbs ground lamb for the ground beef.

RANCH VENISON BURGERS

Use recipe for Ranch Beef Burgers except substitute 1¼ lbs ground venison and ¼ lb ground beef suet for the ground beef.

EASY CHILI PIZZAS

6 large split hamburger buns
Two 15-oz cans chili con carne (without beans)
1 cup chopped onion
1 cup chopped green bell pepper
salt
One 8-oz package mozzarella cheese, shredded

Preheat oven to 375°. Place the 12 halves of the buns on a baking sheet, cut side up.

Spoon undiluted chili generously on bun halves and spread over top. Distribute chopped onion and green pepper over chili. Sprinkle each with salt. Place in preheated oven for 10 minutes. Remove and spread cheese over each bun half.

Return to oven until hot and bubbly. Allow 2 halves each for 6 people.

HERBED LAMB SHANKS

6 lamb shanks
1 cup beef broth (or 1 beef bouillon cube dissolved in 1 cup water)
¼ cup red table wine
One 8-oz can tomato juice
¼ cup dark brown sugar
1 medium onion, chopped
2 medium cloves garlic, minced
2 Tbsps dry parsley flakes
1 tsp dill
¼ tsp oregano
¼ tsp rosemary
½ tsp salt
½ tsp lemon pepper
dash Tabasco

Preheat oven to 325°. Arrange shanks in a roaster, side by side. Combine all other ingredients in a saucepan and mix with a spoon. Place over medium heat and cook and stir until hot. Spoon mixture over shanks. Cover roaster with lid and place in preheated oven.

Bake slowly for 45 minutes, turn meat and replace lid. Return to oven and bake 45 minutes more. Turn shanks again and return to oven uncovered. Cook for an additional 45 minutes or until tender. Serves 6.

MINTY LAMB BROIL

8 to 12 lamb chops (allow 2 per person)
1 cup dry white wine
½ cup white crème de menthe liqueur
5½ Tbsps butter
1 clove garlic, crushed
½ tsp salt
¼ tsp lemon pepper

Place chops side by side in large oblong Pyrex dish. Mix wine and liqueur well, pour over meat. Marinate chops for several hours, turning every 30 minutes. Drain meat on paper towels and blot well.

Combine butter, garlic, salt and pepper in a small pan. Heat and stir until butter is melted. Brush chops with butter mixture. Broil or grill on each side to desired doneness. Serves 4 to 6.

STUFFED LEG OF LAMB

One 7- to 8-lb leg of lamb
4 cups bread crumbs
¼ cup chopped parsley

½ tsp salt
⅛ tsp marjoram
⅛ tsp basil
¼ lb butter or margarine
1 cup chopped celery
½ cup chopped onion
1 egg, beaten with ¼ cup of water
1 cup halved white seedless grapes
2 tsps seasoned salt
1 tsp garlic powder
½ tsp lemon pepper

Have butcher remove bone from leg of lamb. In a large mixing bowl, combine bread crumbs, parsley, salt, marjoram and basil. Toss to mix well.

Heat butter in a skillet. Add chopped celery and onion. Sauté slowly for several minutes. Turn into bowl with bread crumb mixture. Add egg/water mixture. Mix well. Stir in grapes.

Stuff lamb leg with mixture (any left over may be baked separately). With lamb cut side up, pull meat up and over stuffing. Secure with skewers or tie with twine. Mix seasoned salt, garlic powder and pepper. Rub evenly on outside of meat.

Transfer stuffed lamb leg to a rack in an open roasting pan. Place in oven preheated to 325°. Roast for 3–3¼ hours. Remove from oven, cover and let stand for 20 minutes before carving. Gravy may be made by using the pan drippings as a base if desired. Serves 8 to 10.

ROAST PORK

One	10x16-inch Brown-In-Bag
1½	Tbsps flour
⅔	cup apple juice
One	4- to 5-lb boneless pork roast
	seasoned salt
	lemon pepper
¼	tsp dill seed
1	tsp dry mustard
5 or 6	ribs celery

Preheat oven to 375°. Shake flour in the Brown-In-Bag and place bag in a shallow pan or baking dish. Pour apple juice into bag and turn to mix well with flour.

Trim excess fat from roast. Rinse in cool water. Rub salt, pepper, dill seed and dry mustard over meat. Place roast inside bag with celery.

Bake in preheated oven for 30 minutes, then lower heat to 325°. Bake for 2½–3 hours until meat is tender and browned. Remove from bag. If not serving immediately, wrap roast in foil. Serves 6.

Note: Gravy may be made by using roast drippings as a base after skimming off excess fat.

SPARERIBS AND SAUERKRAUT

3 to 4	lbs spareribs
	salt
	pepper
Two	16-oz cans sauerkraut
	water as directed

Drop ribs into a large pot of salted boiling water. Cook until nearly tender. Drain.

Transfer meat to broiler. Salt and pepper lightly. Brown to golden, turn and brown other side.

Place sauerkraut in a Dutch oven and spread with a fork. Add 2 cups water.

Separate ribs into serving-size pieces. Place ribs over sauerkraut. Bring mixture to a brisk boil over high heat. Cover with lid, reduce heat to low. Simmer for 30 minutes. Serves 6.

BARBECUED PINEAPPLE SPARERIBS

½ cup catsup
One 8-oz can crushed pineapple
Three 8-oz cans tomato sauce
4 tsps liquid smoke
2 Tbsps Worcestershire sauce
¼ cup brown sugar
1 cup pineapple juice
5 lbs meaty spareribs

Make sauce by combining all ingredients except ribs in a large pot or Dutch oven. Bring to boil over medium heat. Reduce heat and simmer, uncovered. Stir sauce often to prevent sticking to bottom of pot. When mixture is the consistency of catsup, remove from burner. Set aside, uncovered.

Remove any excess fat from meat. Cut ribs into serving-size pieces. Place in a large pot and cover with water. Bring to a full boil, reduce heat to low and place lid on pot. Simmer ribs for 45 minutes or until barely tender. Drain off and discard liquid.

Spread ribs out in a large shallow pan. Spoon sauce over them. Place in oven preheated to 400° and bake until lightly browned on top. Turn ribs with a meat fork and spoon sauce on other side. Bake until lightly browned on top.

Good with baked potatoes or ears of corn and a tossed green salad. Serves 4 to 6.

Note: Leftover sauce will keep well in refrigerator. Place in jar and screw lid on tightly.

PORK STEAKS IN BROWN GRAVY

6 large cubed pork steaks
flour and salt for dredging
4 Tbsps cooking oil
4½ Tbsps flour
3 Tbsps fat meat drippings or browned melted butter
1 tsp salt
¼ tsp lemon pepper
2 cups meat broth (or 2 bouillon cubes dissolved in 2 cups water)
3 Tbsps grated fresh or bottled horseradish
finely chopped parsley

Lightly dust each side of steaks with flour and salt. Heat oil in a heavy skillet. Fry steaks to a golden brown on each side. Keep meat warm while making sauce.

Place flour in a small skillet over medium heat. Stir until evenly brown. Measure and heat drippings in skillet where steaks were cooked. Add browned flour, salt and pepper. Mix well.

Add ½ cup of broth. Stir vigorously. Add remaining broth and horseradish. Cook and stir constantly until thick and smooth. If a thinner gravy is desired, add hot water.

Transfer steaks to a large hot platter. Spoon gravy over meat. Sprinkle parsley over top. Serve with grits and hot biscuits. Makes 6 portions.

ZESTY PORK CHOPS

6 large loin pork chops, 1½ inches thick
3 Tbsps cooking oil
2 cups water
½ tsp lemon pepper
1 tsp seasoned salt
1 tsp sugar
¼ cup catsup
2 tsps yellow prepared mustard
1 cup finely chopped onion
½ cup chopped dill pickle

Place oil in a large electric skillet and heat to sizzling. Sauté chops to a golden brown on each side. Drain off fat and discard.

Mix water, pepper, salt, sugar, catsup and mustard. Pour over chops in skillet. Sprinkle onion and pickle over chops. Bring liquid to a full boil. Reduce heat to low. Place lid tightly on skillet.

Simmer until liquid is cooked down and very thick like catsup. Transfer chops to a hot platter. Spoon pan drippings over chops. Good with baked or whipped potatoes. Serves 6.

BAKED STUFFED PORK CHOPS

Have butcher cut 6 choice pork chops 1½ inches thick (about ¾ lb each) and slit a pocket in each for stuffing.

4 slices bread
½ cup finely chopped celery
2 Tbsps finely chopped parsley
¼ cup raisins
½ cup applesauce
salt
nutmeg

Dry out bread in oven set at 200° (do not brown). Cool and cut into ¼-inch cubes. Place in a bowl and toss with the celery, parsley and raisins. Add applesauce and mix well.

Stuff pockets of pork chops with the stuffing and skewer together with wooden toothpicks. Sprinkle each side of the chops lightly with salt and nutmeg.

Loosely wrap each chop in foil and place in a large shallow pan (do not crowd together). Bake in oven preheated to 350° for 1½ hours. Serve with applesauce. Serves 6.

PORK CHOPS AND APPLES IN RAISIN SAUCE

6 large rib pork chops (about 1 inch thick)
3 Tbsps vegetable oil
water as directed
4 large cooking apples
¾ cup raisins
½ tsp salt
¼ cup sugar
1 Tbsp lemon juice

1 cup orange juice
1 Tbsp cornstarch mixed with ¼ cup water

Lightly salt each side of pork chops. Heat oil in a large skillet. Sauté meat in hot oil until golden on each side. Drain on absorbent paper. Discard oil from skillet.

Place 1 cup water and the chops in skillet. Bring to a rolling boil over medium heat. Cover with lid and reduce heat to low. Simmer meat slowly for 25–30 minutes. Add small amount of hot water when and if needed.

Peel and core apples. Cut each apple into 6 wedges and arrange on top of chops. Cover with lid and simmer until apples are tender but not mushy.

Combine raisins, salt, sugar, lemon juice, orange juice and ¾ cup water in a large saucepan. Boil over medium heat until raisins are puffed up and tender. Reduce heat. Stir cornstarch/water mixture and add to raisins, stirring constantly. When thickened, remove from heat.

Arrange pork chops and apples on a large hot platter and spoon raisin sauce over them. Serves 6.

HAM AND TANGY RED-EYE GRAVY

Two 1-inch-thick center-cut slices cured ham
¼ lb salt pork
¼ cup water
1¼ cups strong perked coffee
dash cayenne pepper
dash paprika
dash Tabasco

Cut each slice of ham into 3 equal pieces. Set aside.

Wash salt pork well to remove all traces of salt. Slice thinly. Fry in a heavy skillet over low heat until the grease has been rendered. Discard the sliced meat.

Fry ham slices in the fat, browning on each side. Hold skillet lid in one hand and pour water into skillet with the other. Quickly place lid over skillet to avoid spattering. Allow to cook until sizzling stops.

Place ham on a hot platter and keep warm. Add coffee, cayenne, paprika and Tabasco to skillet. Bring to a boil. Scrape bottom of skillet well with a spoon as mixture boils for a minute or two. Pour into gravy boat. Serve with the ham and hot biscuits. Makes 6 portions.

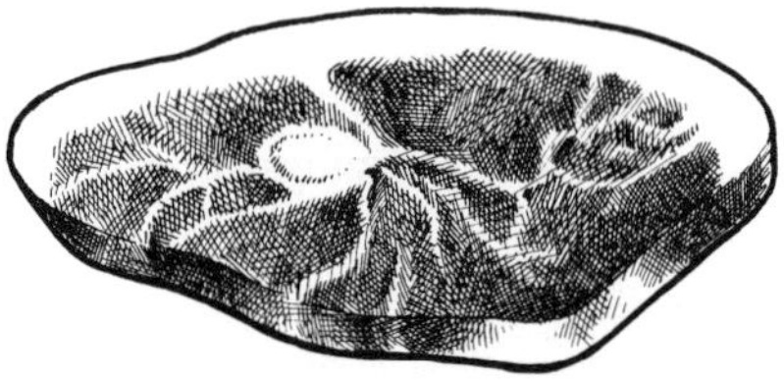

BAKED HAM AND APPLES

2 center cuts of precooked ham, 1 inch thick
6 cooking apples
cinnamon

Cut each slice of ham into 3 equal pieces and place pieces side by side in a large baking pan. Peel and core apples, then cut into 8 slices each. Spread apple slices over the ham. Sprinkle with cinnamon.

Cover pan tightly with foil. Bake in oven preheated to 350° for 50 minutes or until apples are well done. Makes 6 portions.

DEVILED HAM OVER RICE

1 cup thinly sliced celery
½ cup chopped onion
1½ Tbsps peanut or olive oil
One 10½-oz can condensed cream of mushroom soup

¼ cup cooking sherry
2 tsps prepared yellow mustard
¼ tsp dillweed
1 lb fully cooked ham cut into thin strips (about 3 cups)
One 4-oz can sliced mushrooms, drained
¾ cup dairy sour cream
3 cups cooked hot rice
paprika
parsley

Sauté celery and onion in oil over low heat until onion is tender but not brown. Add soup, sherry, mustard and dill. Cook and stir until smooth.

Blend in ham and mushrooms. Heat thoroughly. Add sour cream and heat, but do not allow to boil. Spoon over rice. Garnish with paprika and parsley. Serves 4 to 6.

PAN-BARBECUED WIENERS

2 lbs wieners
1½ cups tomato sauce
½ cup pineapple juice
½ cup catsup
1 tsp liquid smoke
1 Tbsp Worcestershire sauce
¼ tsp onion powder
¼ cup water

Combine all ingredients except the wieners in a large iron skillet. Place over medium heat. Bring sauce to a full boil, add wieners. Stir until all are coated with sauce.

Turn burner to low. Cook and stir occasionally until sauce is the consistency of catsup.

Very good with beans. Also delicious on cooked rice, macaroni or other pasta. Serves 8 to 10.

DADDY'S BATTER-FRIED SALT PORK

1 lb sliced salt side pork
3 Tbsps cooking oil
1 egg
¾ cup milk
1 cup flour
¼ tsp salt

Rinse each slice of pork thoroughly and remove all traces of salt. Pat slices dry. Set aside.

Place oil in a large heavy skillet over medium heat. As oil heats, make batter. In a small bowl, beat egg until lemon colored. Stir in milk. Add flour and salt. Beat well to a thick paste.

When skillet is hot, dip 1 slice of pork at a time in the batter and place in skillet. Cook 3 or 4 slices only at a time, do not crowd. Cook to a golden brown on each side. Remove to absorbent paper. Continue until all slices are cooked.

Serve as you would bacon. Enough for 4 to 6.

LIVER LOAF

2 lbs beef, calf or pork liver, in one piece
liver broth as directed
3 eggs
1½ tsps seasoned salt
2 Tbsps steak sauce
¼ lb bulk pork sausage
2 cups fine bread crumbs

Grease bottom of a 9x5x3-inch loaf pan and set aside. Pour 2 quarts of water into a large pot. Bring to a rolling boil over high heat. Drop in liver. When boiling resumes, turn burner to low. Simmer liver for 20 minutes. Remove liver from the broth.

Strain off ¾ cup of the liquid for use in the loaf. Discard remaining broth. Grind cooked liver and place in a large mixing bowl with the measured broth. Mix with a spoon. Allow to cool to room temperature.

Beat eggs, salt and steak sauce together. Stir into liver mixture. Add sausage and bread crumbs. Work with hands, kneading until completely blended. Pack firmly in prepared loaf pan.

Bake in oven preheated to 400° for 20 minutes. Lower heat to 325° and bake on bottom shelf for 1¼ hours. Let loaf stand in pan for 10 minutes before turning out. This may be served cold for sandwiches or cold cuts or may be served hot with your favorite sauce or gravy.

OVEN-BARBECUED BEEF LIVER

2 Tbsps cooking oil
2 to 2½ lbs beef liver sliced ¼ inch thick
salt
pepper
½ cup chopped onion
2 Tbsps wine vinegar
1 Tbsp Worcestershire sauce
1 Tbsp brown sugar
¼ tsp lemon pepper
1 tsp prepared mustard
¼ cup catsup
½ tsp chili powder
¾ cup water

Heat oil in skillet. Sauté liver seasoned with salt and pepper to light brown on all sides. Remove from skillet and set aside.

Sauté chopped onion in the oil until partially tender. Add all other ingredients except liver. Stir well to blend. Bring to a rolling boil. Reduce heat, cover and simmer slowly for 5 minutes.

Arrange liver in an oblong baking dish. Spoon sauce over liver. Cover with foil. Bake in oven preheated to 325° for 45 minutes. Serves 6.

LIVER AND ONIONS

2 lbs thinly sliced baby beef, beef or pork liver
½ cup flour
3 Tbsps cooking oil
2 large onions, sliced and pulled apart into rings
1½ tsps salt
½ tsp pepper
1 cup water, more if needed

Dredge liver in flour. Set aside. Sauté onions in 1½ tablespoons of the oil in a large skillet over low heat. When onions are wilted down but not browned, remove from skillet and set aside.

Pour remaining oil into skillet. Over medium heat, brown liver slices, turn and brown other side. Sprinkle with salt and pepper. Add onions and water.

Bring to a boil over medium heat. Lower heat and cover tightly with lid. Simmer slowly until onions are tender and gravy has thickened. Place on a hot platter. Serve with hot fluffy biscuits and with strips of crisp fried bacon if you wish. Serves 6.

CREAMED CHICKEN LIVERS

2 lbs whole chicken livers
flour and salt for dusting livers
cooking oil
5 Tbsps butter or rendered chicken fat
5 Tbsps flour
1 tsp salt
¼ tsp white pepper
dash cayenne pepper
2½ cups milk

Divide each liver in half. Salt and dust each piece lightly with flour. Shake off excess. Heat a small amount of oil in a skillet until hot but not smoking. Add livers and lightly brown on each side. Transfer to absorbent paper and set aside.

In a Dutch oven, melt butter or chicken fat. Add flour, salt, pepper and cayenne. Lower heat. Stir vigorously to mix. Return heat to medium. Add milk, about ¼ of the amount at a time, stirring constantly. Cook and stir until thickened. Add chicken livers. Cook and stir for 2 or 3 minutes.

If sauce is too thick, it may be thinned to desired consistency by adding a small amount of milk at a time. This dish is great for breakfast, brunch, lunch, dinner or supper. Spoon over large hot fluffy biscuits, toast or rice. Serves 6.

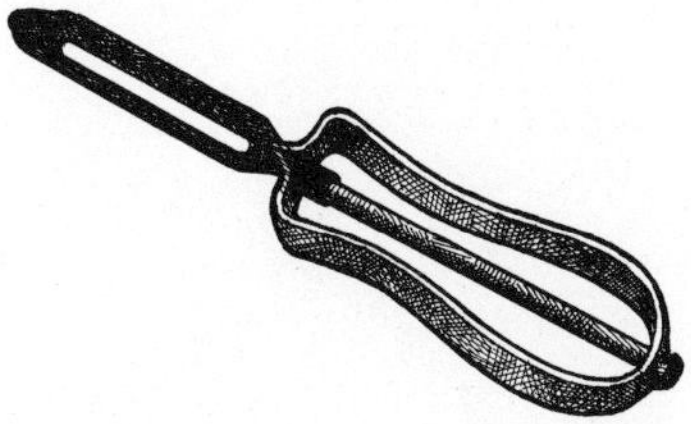

SAUTÉED SEASONED CHICKEN LIVERS

2 lbs chicken livers
salt
pepper
¼ cup flour
4 Tbsps butter or margarine
1 Tbsp vinegar or lemon juice
2 Tbsps red table wine
2 Tbsps chopped parsley
2 Tbsps snipped chives
2 Tbsps water
1 Tbsp bacon drippings
2 slices crisp fried bacon, crumbled

Salt and pepper livers and dust lightly with flour. Heat butter in a heavy skillet to very hot. Add livers and sauté over medium heat for about 3 minutes on each side. Remove to platter and keep hot.

To the same skillet, add vinegar, wine, parsley, chives, water and bacon drippings. Stir well and heat until very hot. Pour over livers. Sprinkle crumbled bacon over top. Serve with grits. Makes 6 portions.

FOWL

COUNTRY-FRIED CHICKEN AND CREAM GRAVY

- 4 lbs choice frying-chicken parts
- 2 cups milk
- 1 cup flour
- 1½ tsps salt
- ½ tsp white pepper
- ⅓ cup light cooking oil (or more if needed)

Cream Gravy:

- fat from skillet as directed
- ⅓ cup flour
- 1 tsp salt
- ⅛ tsp white pepper
- 3 cups milk

Rinse chicken pieces and place in a large mixing bowl. Pour milk over chicken. Let soak for 1 hour, turning occasionally.

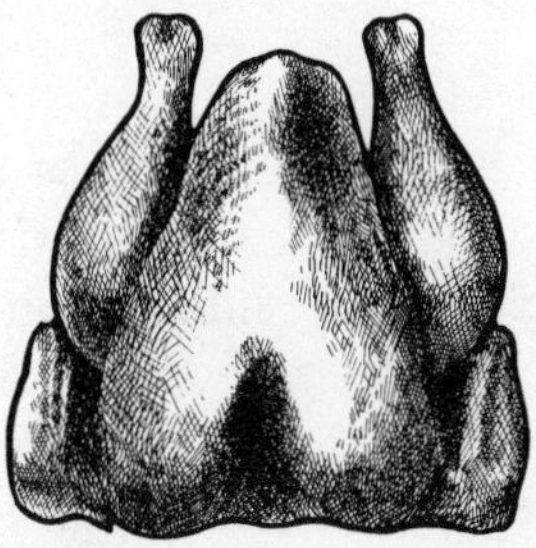

Combine flour, salt and pepper in a plastic bag. Shake well to mix. Shake chicken pieces slightly to remove excess milk. Place 2 or 3 pieces at a time in bag with flour mixture and shake to coat. Arrange coated chicken on wax paper on counter. Continue until all pieces are coated.

Heat cooking oil over medium heat in a large heavy iron skillet until hot. Place chicken in hot oil, but do not crowd. Cook until brown on bottom, turn and brown other side. When brown, lower heat and cook 5 minutes, turn and cook 5 minutes more. Remove to absorbent paper. After draining, place pieces in warm oven while making gravy.

Measure oil left in skillet to ⅓ cup. If that much does not remain, add enough to measure ⅓ cup. Pour back into skillet. Place over medium heat until oil is hot. Add flour, salt and pepper and cook and mix vigorously with a spoon until smooth. Pour in about ½ of the milk. Cook and stir constantly for 1 or 2 minutes. Add remaining milk. Cook and stir until thick and smooth. If thinner gravy is desired, more milk may be added.

Serve chicken and gravy with hot biscuits. Serves 6.

SEASONED BAKED CHICKEN

3 broiler chickens, halved
seasoned salt
garlic powder
onion powder
pepper
paprika

Rinse chicken halves. Sprinkle each of the seasonings on cut side of chickens, but use garlic powder sparingly.

Place chicken halves cut side down in a large oblong enamelware pan 3 inches deep. Sprinkle seasonings over outer side of chickens. Cover pan tightly with foil. With a toothpick, punch a few small holes near center of pan for venting.

Place on middle shelf in oven preheated to 400°. Cook for 45 minutes. Reduce heat to 350°. Bake for 15–20 minutes or until chicken is tender and lightly browned. Serves 6.

GRINGO CHICKEN

3 to 4	lbs cut-up frying chicken
	salt and pepper
	cooking oil as directed
Two	8-oz cans tomato sauce
1	cup water
One	4-oz can chopped green chili peppers
2	Tbsps chili powder
1/8	tsp garlic powder
2	large onions, sliced
2	large green bell peppers, seeded and sliced

Rinse chicken and dry with towel. Salt and pepper each piece lightly. Pour a small amount of oil in a large skillet and heat. Over high heat, brown chicken quickly on all sides. Remove from burner.

Combine tomato sauce, water, chili peppers, chili powder and garlic powder. Mix with a spoon.

Arrange prepared chicken in a large roaster. Place onions and green pepper slices over chicken. Pour tomato sauce over all.

Cover roaster with lid. Bake in oven preheated to 350° for 1½ hours, basting occasionally.

Serve hot with corn bread and beans. Makes 6 portions.

SESAME CHICKEN

1 cup dairy sour cream
½ cup milk
½ tsp salt
½ tsp poultry seasoning
2 cups fine cracker crumbs
¼ cup sesame seed
6 whole frying-chicken breasts
3 Tbsps melted butter or margarine

Beat sour cream, milk, salt and poultry seasoning together with a fork until smooth. Set aside.

Toss cracker crumbs and sesame seed together in another dish, mixing well. Dip chicken in sour cream mixture, then coat well with the crumb mixture.

Grease inside of a 13x9x2-inch baking dish. Arrange chicken parts in dish. Drizzle ½ tablespoon of melted butter over the top of each piece. Bake in oven preheated to 350° until chicken is tender and golden, about 1 hour.

Transfer chicken to hot platter and garnish with sprigs of parsley. Serve with your favorite sauce or gravy. Makes 6 portions.

SMOTHERED CHICKEN

3 to 4 lbs choice frying-chicken parts
1 cup flour mixed with ½ tsp salt
½ cup light cooking oil
1½ tsps celery salt
½ tsp pepper
1 Tbsp snipped chives
2½ cups boiling water

Rinse chicken parts. Place flour mixture in a plastic bag and shake. Coat 2 or 3 pieces of chicken at a time by shaking in bag. Remove to wax paper.

Heat oil in a large heavy skillet. Quickly brown chicken on all sides over high heat. Watch carefully, do not burn. Drain browned chicken on absorbent paper.

Place prepared chicken pieces side by side in a large baking pan or roaster. Combine celery salt, pepper, chives and boiling water and pour over chicken. Place lid or foil over top of pan.

Cook in oven preheated to 350° for 1 hour or until chicken is tender. Serves 6.

TEXICAN CHICKEN

⅓ cup flour
1 Tbsp chili powder
1 tsp salt
½ tsp pepper
⅓ cup light cooking oil
12 pieces (about 2 pounds) choice chicken parts
1 cup chopped onion
1 Tbsp butter or margarine
1½ cups chicken broth
½ cup dry sherry
1 cup chili sauce
½ tsp garlic powder
1 Tbsp corn syrup
½ tsp celery salt

Combine flour, chili powder, salt and pepper. Mix well. Coat chicken pieces with flour mixture. Heat oil in a large heavy skillet to sizzling. Cook chicken in oil to golden brown. Drain on absorbent paper.

In a small skillet, slowly stir-fry onion in butter until tender but not browned. In a large saucepan, combine sautéed onion, broth, sherry, chili sauce, garlic powder, corn syrup and celery salt. Stir well. Bring to a boil over medium heat. Lower heat and simmer for 5 minutes.

Place chicken in a 13x9x2-inch baking dish. Pour hot sauce over chicken. Bake in oven preheated to 350° for 45–50 minutes or until chicken is tender. Serve with rice or noodles. Serves 6.

CHICKEN OR TURKEY CROQUETTES

3 Tbsps rendered chicken fat or melted butter
5 Tbsps flour
¾ tsp salt
¼ tsp lemon pepper
1 cup milk
3 cups (packed) ground cooked chicken or turkey
1 Tbsp snipped chives
2 eggs
3 Tbsps cream
cracker meal
cooking oil

Place fat in small pan. Heat over low burner. Add flour, salt and pepper. Mix thoroughly, taking care not to burn. Add ½ of milk. Stir vigorously and add remaining milk. Cook and stir until very thick. Remove from heat and cool. Cover and refrigerate for 2 hours.

Toss ground chicken and chives in a mixing bowl. Add white sauce. Mix well with hands as for meat loaf. Divide into 6 equal parts. Shape each part into oblong, thick patties.

Beat eggs and cream together. Dip croquettes in egg mixture. Coat with cracker meal. Deep fry in hot oil until golden brown. Drain on absorbent paper.

Serve with creamed peas or your favorite sauce or gravy. Makes 6 large croquettes.

ROAST TURKEY WITH CORN BREAD DRESSING AND GIBLET GRAVY

12- to 14-lb turkey
salt
pepper
Corn bread Dressing (see page 128)

Giblet Gravy:

giblets from turkey
turkey neck
3 cups broth
6 Tbsps flour
salt and pepper to taste
2 hard-cooked eggs, chopped
2 Tbsps finely chopped parsley

Make dressing according to directions and set aside.

Remove neck and giblets from inside turkey. Rinse fowl inside and out. Dry with towel. Salt and pepper outside. Fill inside of neck cavity with dressing. Cover with skin and skewer together. Stuff large cavity.

Fold wing tips across the back of the fowl. Tie legs to the tail. Brush turkey with light cooking oil. Place on cooking rack with breast side up.

Bake in oven preheated to 375° for 1 hour. Lower heat to 325°. Bake for 3½–4 more hours or until bird is tender.

Let stand for 20 minutes before carving.

To make gravy:

Cook giblets and neck by simmering in water. Remove liver

after 15 minutes. Allow neck and other giblets to cook for 1½ hours or until tender.

Chop giblets and meat from neck, taking care to remove all small bones. Measure broth and add enough water to make 3 cups. Place in saucepan.

Blend flour with a small amount of water, making a smooth paste. Add to broth, stirring well. Cook and stir until thickened.

Add chopped giblets, neck meat, chopped eggs, parsley, salt and pepper. Stir well and bring to a slow boil. Remove from heat. Serve with turkey and dressing. Remember to pass the cranberry sauce.

CORN BREAD DRESSING

- 1½ cups chopped celery
- ⅓ cup chopped green onion
- water as directed
- ¼ cup chopped parsley
- 1 tsp poultry seasoning
- 1½ tsps rubbed sage
- 2 cups turkey or chicken broth (or more for desired consistency)
- 6 cups cubed corn bread
- 2 cups cubed biscuits or white bread

Any one or a combination of the following optional ingredients may be added:

- chopped hard cooked eggs
- chopped canned or fresh mushrooms
- canned small oysters

Combine celery and onion in a saucepan. Cover with boiling water and bring to a boil over medium heat. Cook until vegetables are barely tender.

Add parsley and seasonings. Stir, then cook for 1 or 2

minutes. Add broth and stir. Cook to a low boil, then remove from burner.

Place all the bread cubes in a large container, toss to mix. If using any of the optional ingredients, add to bread cubes at this point and toss. While stirring, slowly add broth mixture, blending carefully with a spoon. Add more broth if a softer dressing is desired.

Use as a stuffing for turkey or chicken. Or use as meat accompaniment by browning in a large baking dish in a 325° oven for 10 to 15 minutes.

Serves 6 or more.

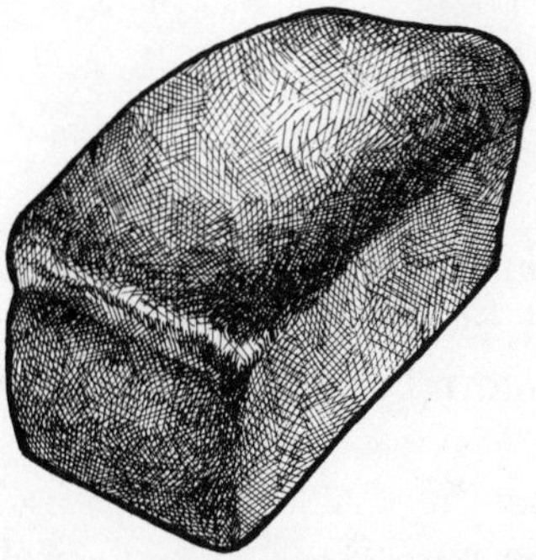

HICKORY-SMOKED TURKEY

10- to 14-lb turkey
salt
lemon pepper
paprika
light cooking oil

Rinse inside and outside of turkey. Dry with a towel. Rub salt, pepper and paprika over outside and inside of bird. Rub with cooking oil.

Start charcoal fire in smoker. Allow to burn 12–18 minutes. Add 8 to 10 hickory chips to fire.

Fill water pan with water and place in smoker. Lay prepared turkey on grill and cover tightly with lid. Do not open smoker during cooking time.

Smoke for 9–11 hours. Fowl is done when drumstick joints move easily. Makes up to 25 servings.

TURKEY LOAF

6 cups (packed) ground or finely minced cooked turkey meat
¾ cup fine cracker meal
¼ cup finely chopped parsley
2 eggs
2 Tbsps milk
½ tsp onion powder
½ tsp celery salt
1 tsp seasoned salt
½ tsp lemon pepper

Combine ground turkey meat, cracker meal and parsley in a large mixing bowl. Beat eggs, milk and seasonings together until frothy and pour into mixing bowl with turkey. Mix well with both hands as for meat loaf.

Lightly grease the inside of a 9x5x3-inch loaf pan. Pack turkey mixture into pan. Bake in oven preheated to 325° for 1¼ hours. Let stand in pan for 10 or 15 minutes. Serve with your favorite sauce or gravy.

Note: This loaf slices better if cooled at room temperature and is then chilled for at least 3 hours in the refrigerator. May be reheated after slicing by wrapping in foil and placing in 350° oven for 20–25 minutes. Turkey Loaf is good served cold in sandwiches and with cold cuts.

TURKEY RICE OLÉ

2 Tbsps butter or meat drippings
1 medium onion, finely chopped
1 medium green bell pepper, finely chopped
1 cup tomato juice

One 16-oz can tomatoes
1½ tsps salt
2 Tbsps chili powder
3 cups (packed) finely diced cooked turkey meat
4 cups cooked rice

Heat butter or drippings in a large skillet. Sauté onion and pepper over low heat until partially tender. Add tomato juice and tomatoes. Cut tomatoes into small pieces. Bring to a full boil over medium heat. Cook until liquid is reduced by half. Add salt and chili powder. Stir well.

Add turkey meat and cooked rice, mixing well with a spoon. Turn into a greased casserole. Bake in oven preheated to 325° for 45 minutes or until liquid is absorbed. Serves 4 to 6.

Note: Chicken or rabbit meat may be substituted for the turkey.

ROAST DUCK

3- to 5-lb duck
salt and pepper to taste
garlic powder
1 small onion, sliced
4 ribs celery, cut into 3-inch lengths
1 bay leaf
3 or 4 sprigs parsley
melted butter

Clean duck thoroughly. Remove excess fat from inside bird. Sprinkle inside and outside with salt and pepper. Sprinkle garlic powder sparingly on outside of duck.

Place other ingredients inside fowl. Brush with melted butter. Place in a roasting pan in oven preheated to 400°.

Cook about 20 minutes per pound (1 hour for 3 pounds; 1 hour and 20 minutes for 4 pounds; 1 hour and 40 minutes for 5 pounds). After roasting 40 minutes, drain fat from pan and turn duck to the other side. Serve with favorite sauce. Serves 2 or 3, according to size of bird.

DUCK IN BING CHERRY SAUCE

One 4- to 5-lb duck cut into serving pieces
salt as directed
3 Tbsps cooking oil
orange juice as directed
1 cup water
1 bay leaf
⅛ tsp marjoram
melted butter or margarine as directed
One 16-oz can Bing cherries in syrup
2 Tbsps cornstarch mixed with ¼ cup water

Lightly salt all sides of duck pieces. Heat oil in a large iron skillet. Lightly brown pieces of duck on each side. Drain off and discard fat. Add 1 cup orange juice, water, bay leaf and marjoram to skillet. Bring to a rolling boil, cover with lid and reduce heat to low. Simmer until duck is just tender. Do not overcook. Drain off liquid and discard bay leaf.

Arrange duck pieces on a baking sheet. Brush with melted butter. Place on bottom shelf of oven preheated to 375°. Bake for 15 minutes, turn pieces and brush with melted butter. Return to oven for another 15 minutes. While duck bakes, make sauce.

Drain syrup from cherries and measure. Add enough orange juice to the syrup to make 1½ cups. Place mixture with cherries in a saucepan. Bring to a boil. Stirring constantly, add cornstarch mixture. Cook and stir until thickened. Remove pan from heat and cover with lid.

Arrange duck on a large hot platter. Pour cherry sauce over duck. Serves 4 to 6.

DUCK WITH ORANGE STUFFING

One 5-lb duck
1 cup orange juice
½ tsp salt
½ tsp poultry seasoning
4 cups lightly toasted stale bread cubes
4 navel oranges, peeled and membranes removed
2 cups chopped celery
2 eggs, beaten until frothy

For basting:

1 cup orange juice
½ cup cooking oil
1 tsp salt

Combine orange juice, salt and poultry seasoning in a small saucepan. Heat and stir until well mixed and hot. Place bread cubes in a large mixing bowl. Stir while pouring hot juice mixture over bread cubes. Let stand for 20 minutes, stirring occasionally.

Coarsely chop prepared oranges. Add to bread mixture and add celery and eggs. Mix well. Spoon stuffing into cavity of duck. Skewer skin together. Place in a shallow roasting pan and into oven preheated to 325°.

For basting, combine orange juice, oil and salt in a small saucepan. Over medium heat, stir until hot. Baste duck with hot mixture every 25–30 minutes. Roast for 2½ hours or until tender. Serves 6.

FRUITED STUFFED GOOSE

One	10- to 12-lb goose
8	slices dry bread, cut into cubes and lightly browned in oven
1½	cups chopped celery
3	apples, cored and chopped
1½	cups chopped pitted prunes
1	cup coarsely chopped walnuts
1	Tbsp poppy seed
One	12-oz can apricot nectar

If bird is frozen, defrost thoroughly.

Toss bread, celery, apples, prunes, nuts and poppy seed together in a mixing bowl. Add apricot nectar and mix well. Cover and let stand for 1 hour, stirring occasionally.

Preheat oven to 325°. Prick goose with a fork thoroughly all over so fat will cook out. Lightly salt outside of goose. Spoon stuffing into cavity. Skewer skin together.

Place stuffed goose on a rack in a shallow roasting pan. Cook slowly in preheated oven for 4 hours or until tender. Do not oil or baste while cooking. Spoon off fat from bottom of pan occasionally as bird cooks.

Serve with sauce or gravy of your choice. Serves 6.

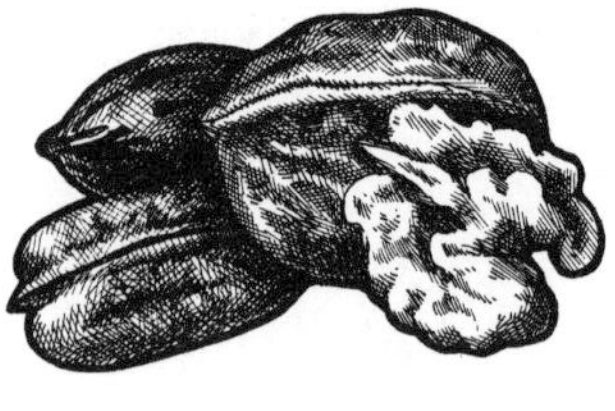

STUFFED ROAST SQUABS

4 cups fresh bread crumbs
¼ lb mushrooms, cleaned and chopped
½ cup chopped celery
3 Tbsps chopped parsley
1 Tbsp snipped chives
1 tsp salt
4 Tbsps butter, melted
⅔ cup orange juice
6 1-lb squabs, cleaned

For basting:

¼ lb butter
¼ tsp rubbed sage
¼ tsp savory
½ tsp salt
¼ cup orange juice

Combine crumbs, mushrooms, celery, parsley and chives in a mixing bowl. Toss thoroughly. Add salt, melted butter and orange juice. Mix well.

Stuff squabs with mixture. Skewer openings closed. With breast sides up, place on rack in a shallow pan. Place basting ingredients in a saucepan and heat. Spoon over the birds.

Place squabs in oven preheated to 450°. Bake 10 minutes and baste again. Lower heat to 350°. Cook, basting with drippings every 10 minutes, for 40 minutes. Test with fork for doneness. If needed, cook an additional 10 minutes. Serves 6.

SEA FOOD

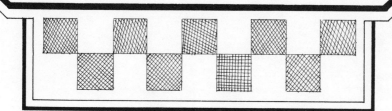

FRIED CATFISH

2 lbs catfish fillets
2 eggs
1 tsp salt
3 Tbsps milk
1 cup cornmeal
3 Tbsps flour
cooking oil

If fish is frozen, defrost thoroughly. Dry fish with paper towels. Spread wax paper on counter.

Beat eggs, salt and milk together until frothy. In another dish, mix cornmeal and flour.

Dip fillets one at a time in egg mixture, then coat with cornmeal. Place each prepared fillet side by side on wax paper.

Allow to dry for 5 minutes, turn each fillet over and allow other side to dry for 5 minutes.

Heat oil to 365° in deep fryer. Lay 2 or 3 fillets (do not crowd) inside frying basket and immerse in hot oil. Cook to a golden brown. Drain on absorbent paper. Continue until all of fish is fried.

Serve with tartar sauce and hush puppies. Makes 6 portions.

FISH WITH SEASONED BUTTER

1½ lbs fish fillets of your choice
Seasoned Butter (see page 87)
fine dry bread crumbs

If fish is frozen, defrost thoroughly. Dry fish well with a towel. Spread seasoned butter on one side of each fillet. Place in 13x9x2-inch baking dish, side by side with buttered side up.

Place on top shelf of oven preheated to 350°. Cook for 15 minutes. Remove from oven. Turn fillets carefully with a spatula. Spread with seasoned butter. Sprinkle with bread crumbs.

Return fillets to oven. Cook 15–20 minutes more or until fish flakes easily with a fork. Serves 6.

BUTTERMILK FRIED FISH FILLETS

2 to 3 lbs fresh or frozen fish fillets
1½ cups buttermilk
1½ cups biscuit mix
½ tsp salt
¼ tsp lemon pepper
½ cup cooking oil (or more if needed)

If fish is frozen, defrost thoroughly. Wipe dry. Cut into serving-size pieces. Pour buttermilk over fish in a bowl. Combine dry ingredients in a shallow dish and mix well.

Pour oil into an iron skillet. Place over medium heat. One at a time, coat fish well with buttermilk, then coat with dry ingredients. When oil is hot, drop one piece at a time into skillet.

Cook until brown on bottom, turn and brown. Drain on absorbent paper. Serve with lemon wedges and hush puppies. Serves 6.

SALMON STEAKS

6 salmon steaks (about 2 lbs), 1 inch thick
6 Tbsps butter, melted
2 Tbsps finely chopped parsley
⅛ tsp onion powder
1 Tbsp lemon juice

Arrange salmon steaks side by side in a shallow pan. Combine all other ingredients, mixing well.

Spoon ½ of butter mixture over steaks. Place pan under broiler. Cook 6 minutes. Remove from broiler and turn steaks carefully. Spoon remaining butter over steaks and return to broiler.

Cook another 6–8 minutes until fish flakes easily with fork.

Serve with tartar sauce and hush puppies. Makes 6 portions.

SALMON CROQUETTES

One 15½-oz can salmon (preferably pink or red)
2 eggs
1 Tbsp lemon juice
¼ cup finely minced onion
¼ cup finely chopped parsley
¾ cup cracker meal
equal amounts of all-purpose flour and cornmeal for dredging
cooking oil

Drain liquid from salmon. Place fish in a mixing bowl and mash (bones and all) with a fork. Add eggs and lemon juice. Mix thoroughly. Add onion, parsley and cracker meal.

With hands, work mixture as for meat loaf, distributing all ingredients evenly. Pack down in bowl, cover with plastic wrap. Refrigerate for 2 or 3 hours. (May be left overnight.)

Shape mixture into 6 croquettes. Dredge with flour/cornmeal mixture (or cracker meal). Fry in hot deep fat to a golden brown. Drain on absorbent paper. Serve with tartar sauce. Makes 6 croquettes.

SALMON LOAF

Two 15-oz cans red or pink salmon, drained
3 eggs, beaten
¼ cup milk
½ tsp lemon pepper
1½ cups (packed) fine bread crumbs
¼ cup finely chopped parsley
¼ cup finely minced green onion

Flake salmon finely into a mixing bowl. Add eggs, milk and pepper. Mix with a spoon. Add bread crumbs, parsley and green onion. Mix well with hands as for meat loaf.

Turn into a greased 9x5x3-inch loaf pan. Bake in oven preheated to 350° for 50–55 minutes or until wooden toothpick inserted into the center of loaf comes out clean.

Let stand 10 minutes before turning out of pan. Serves 6.

FRIED FROGS' LEGS

6 cups water
½ lemon, sliced
1 tsp salt
12 pairs large frogs' legs
1 egg, beaten
¾ cup milk
¾ tsp seasoned salt
⅛ tsp lemon pepper
1 cup flour
½ cup cornmeal
cooking oil as directed

Bring water, lemon slices and salt to a rolling boil in a large pot. Drop in frogs' legs. Return water to boil and cook for 5 minutes.

Stir egg, milk, seasoned salt and pepper together. Add flour and cornmeal. Beat with a spoon until thoroughly mixed.

Pour cooking oil 1 inch deep into a large iron skillet or Dutch oven. Heat to very hot but not smoking. Dip one frog leg at a time in batter and place in hot oil.

Fry a few legs at a time. Do not overcrowd. Cook to a golden brown, turn and brown other side. Drain on absorbent paper. Continue until all legs have been cooked. Serves 6.

JAMBALAYA

Two	16-oz cans stewed tomatoes
One	15-oz can tomato sauce
2	medium onions, cut into chunks
1	large green bell pepper, cored, seeded and cut into chunks
1	large red bell pepper, cored, seeded and cut into chunks
2	medium carrots, sliced into thin rounds
1½	cups thinly sliced celery
½	lb stick salami, cut into ½-inch cubes
2	cloves garlic, finely minced
1	Tbsp cracked or coarse-ground pepper
⅛	tsp cayenne pepper
½	tsp rubbed sage
1	Tbsp sugar
2	tsps salt
1	lb cooked, shelled and deveined shrimp
5	cups cooked rice, hot
	water as directed

Place 2 cups of water in a 5-quart pot. Add tomatoes, tomato sauce, onions, peppers, carrots and celery, salami and garlic.

Bring to a full boil over medium heat. Reduce heat and place lid on pot. Simmer until vegetables are tender. Add pepper, cayenne, sage, sugar, salt and 1 cup of additional water.

Bring to rolling boil. Cook mixture uncovered over medium heat, stirring occasionally, for 15 minutes. Add cooked shrimp, stir to mix. Return to boiling. Cook 2 minutes and remove from heat.

Stir in hot cooked rice. Mix well. Place lid on pot and let stand for about 15 minutes. With pieces of hot buttered French bread and a green salad, this makes a full meal. Serves 6.

Note: Any cooked boned meat, fowl or fish may be used in this recipe in place of or with the shrimp.

SEAFOOD GUMBO

½ cup peanut or light vegetable oil
3 ribs celery, chopped
1 large onion, chopped
½ cup chopped green bell pepper
3 cloves garlic, chopped
½ cup all-purpose flour
water as directed
2 cups cut fresh okra or one 10-oz package frozen cut okra
One 16-oz can tomatoes
3 Tbsps dry parsley flakes
1 tsp pepper
2 tsps salt
¼ tsp hot pepper sauce
One 8- to 12-oz package frozen shelled crab meat, defrosted
1 lb fresh or frozen raw medium shrimp, defrosted
1 pint small shucked oysters
cooked rice

Heat oil in a large skillet. Sauté celery, onion, green pepper and garlic, stirring constantly until vegetables are almost tender.

Add flour and stir constantly until mixture is a deep brown, but do not let it burn. Slowly add 4 cups of water, stirring constantly. Stir until mixture is smooth and thickened.

Transfer mixture to a 5- or 6-quart pot. Add 3 cups boiling water, cut okra, tomatoes and parsley flakes. Place pot over medium heat and bring mixture to a full boil. Reduce heat to low and simmer slowly for 45 minutes.

Add pepper, salt, pepper sauce, crab meat, shrimp and oysters. Stir well to blend. Place pot over high heat until boiling. Reduce heat to low and simmer 10 minutes. Spoon gumbo over hot cooked rice. Serves 6.

FRIED OYSTERS

Breaded Fried Oysters:

1 pint shucked oysters
cracker meal
2 eggs
½ tsp salt
1 Tbsp milk

Roll each oyster in cracker meal to coat and place on wax paper on flat surface. Do not stack.

Beat eggs, salt and milk together, mixing well. Dip an oyster at a time into the egg mixture, then coat with cracker meal. Continue until all have been coated with egg, then meal.

Deep fry oysters a few at a time to a golden brown. Drain on absorbent paper. Serves 2.

Batter-Fried Oysters:

1 pint shucked oysters
flour and cornstarch for dredging
⅔ cup all-purpose flour
½ tsp salt
½ tsp baking soda
⅔ cup buttermilk
1 egg

Dredge each oyster lightly in a mixture of flour and cornstarch. Spread oysters on wax paper on a flat surface. Do not stack.

Make batter by sifting the measured flour, salt and soda together. Beat buttermilk and eggs together and combine with dry ingredients. Beat to a smooth paste.

Dip an oyster at a time in the batter and drop into deep hot fat. Fry oysters a few at a time. Continue until all are golden brown. Drain on absorbent paper as they are removed from pan. Serves 2.

Cornmeal Fried Oysters:

1 pint shucked oysters
1 cup yellow cornmeal mixed with ½ tsp salt

Dredge each oyster in cornmeal mixture, coating well. As they are coated, spread oysters on wax paper on a flat surface; let dry for 30 minutes. Deep fry oysters a few at a time to a golden brown. Drain on absorbent paper. Serves 2.

DRUNK BUTTERFLY SHRIMP

2 lbs fresh or frozen large whole raw shrimp, shelled and deveined
Beer Batter (see page 181)
cooking oil

From the underside of each shrimp, slit almost through to the top of the back. Fold out, butterfly fashion. Blot liquid from shrimp with towel. Make Beer Batter.

Pour cooking oil 1 inch deep in an iron skillet. Place over medium heat until oil sizzles when a drop of water is added. Dip shrimp one at a time in the batter, coating well. Place in the hot oil. Continue until skillet is filled with shrimp but not crowded.

Cook shrimp to a light golden brown, turning as needed for uniform browning. Drain on absorbent paper. Continue until all are cooked. Serve with your favorite sauce or dip. Serves 6.

MEAT ACCOMPANIMENTS

ROLLED DUMPLINGS

3	cups self-rising flour
½	cup vegetable shortening
1	cup cold milk
2½	quarts broth from stewing beef, pork or chicken (only slightly salted)
2	tsps snipped chives (optional)
1	Tbsp finely chopped parsley (optional)
⅛	tsp white or black pepper
One	5⅓-oz can evaporated milk

In a mixing bowl cut shortening into flour with a pastry knife until mixture is the texture of cornmeal. Stir in milk a little at a time to form a stiff dough.

Divide into two equal parts. Place half the dough on a piece of floured wax paper. Sprinkle small amount of flour over top. Shape into a rectangle. Place more wax paper over top. Roll with rolling pin to the thickness of pie crust. Cut into strips 1x3 inches. Set aside.

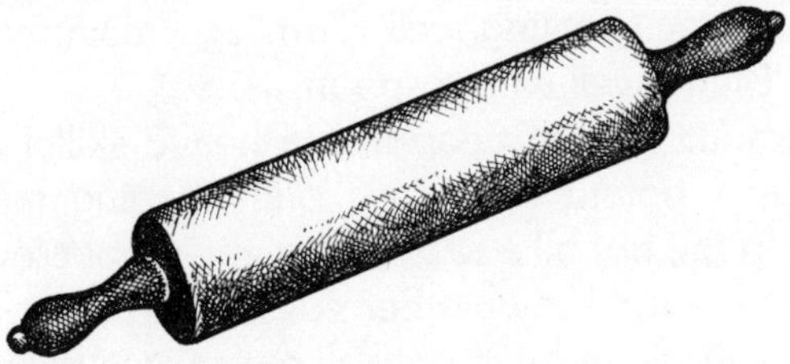

On another strip of wax paper follow same procedure to prepare remaining half of dough. Allow cut dumplings to dry for 30 minutes.

Meantime combine broth, chives, parsley and pepper in a 6- to 8-quart pot. Bring to a rolling boil over high heat. Drop dumplings one at a time into boiling broth. When full boil resumes, heat evaporated milk in a small saucepan to scalding. Pour over dumplings.

Place lid on pot and turn heat to low. Simmer for 15–18 minutes or until dumplings are no longer doughy. Serve with chicken, beef or pork. Serves 6.

RANCHO POTATO PANCAKES

2 lbs small potatoes
1 medium onion, grated
½ cup grated green bell pepper
2 eggs
1½ tsps salt
½ tsp pepper
5 Tbsps flour
cooking oil

Cook unpeeled potatoes in boiling water until barely tender. Drain off water and remove skins from potatoes. Set aside until cold.

Combine onion and green pepper in a large mixing bowl. Grate potatoes coarsely and toss well with onion and green pepper.

In a small bowl, beat eggs with salt and pepper. Add flour, 1 tablespoon at a time, beating well. Turn egg mixture into a bowl with potatoes. Blend well with a spoon.

Pour oil about ½ inch deep into a heavy skillet and heat to sizzling. For each potato cake, use one heaping tablespoon of mixture. Place in the hot oil a few at a time. Do not crowd. Cook to golden brown, turn and brown other sides. Drain well on absorbent paper. Keep hot in warm oven until all pancakes are made. Serves 4 to 6.

MASHED POTATOES AU GRATIN

4 or 5 large potatoes (russets)
¾ cup half-and-half
4 Tbsps butter
1½ tsps salt
½ tsp white pepper
1½ cups shredded mild Cheddar cheese (or other type of cheese if preferred)
paprika

Peel and quarter potatoes. Place in a pot, cover with water and boil until very tender. Drain off water and cover pot with lid.

In a small saucepan, combine half-and-half, butter, salt and pepper. Heat until butter is melted and mixture is steaming. Mash potatoes well with a potato masher. Add hot liquid mixture. Beat with a large spoon until well blended and fluffy.

Turn mixture into a large buttered baking dish. Sprinkle with cheese, then paprika. Bake in oven preheated to 350° for 20–25 minutes. Serves 4 to 6.

BROWNED PARSLEY POTATOES

2 lbs small red new potatoes (1½ inches in diameter)
¼ lb (1 stick) butter or margarine
salt
pepper
½ cup finely chopped parsley

Scrub potatoes with a vegetable brush. In a large pot, cover unpeeled potatoes with water. Boil until just tender. Drain off water and remove potato skins. Salt and pepper the potatoes.

Heat butter in a large heavy skillet. Over medium heat, brown potatoes well in the butter, rolling them occasionally until they are evenly browned all over.

Place potatoes in serving dish and pour butter from skillet over them. Sprinkle parsley on top. Serves 6.

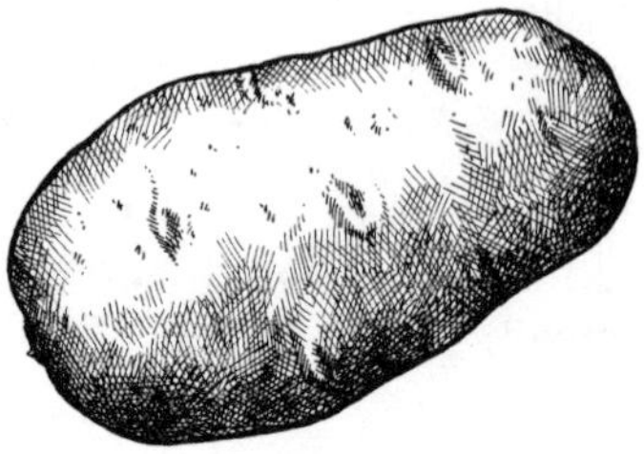

BAKED POTATOES WITH CHEESE SAUCE TOPPING

- 3 extra-large russet potatoes
- ½ lb American cheese, shredded
- 2 Tbsps cream
- 2 Tbsps minced onion
- 1 Tbsp chopped parsley
- dash cayenne pepper
- dash white pepper
- 3 slices crisp fried bacon, crushed

Scrub potatoes with a vegetable brush. Wrap each potato separately in foil and place on top rack of oven preheated to 400°.

Bake for 1½ hours. Test by sticking a fork into the center of each potato. If not completely done, cook additional 15 minutes and test again.

Combine all other ingredients except bacon in top of double boiler. Place top on bottom pan containing boiling water over medium heat. Cook and stir cheese mixture until melted and bubbly. Remove from heat.

Cut potatoes in half lengthwise. Place cut side up in a shallow baking pan. Spoon cheese sauce over potato halves. Sprinkle crumbled bacon over tops. Place under broiler for 1 or 2 minutes. Serves 6.

STUFFED BAKED POTATOES

6 large uniform russet potatoes
One 8-oz package cream cheese, softened
½ cup mayonnaise or dairy sour cream
1 tsp prepared yellow mustard
½ cup cream
1½ tsps salt
¼ tsp white pepper
¼ cup finely chopped parsley
2 Tbsps snipped chives

Scrub potatoes clean and wrap each in foil. Bake in oven preheated to 400° for 1¼–1½ hours until fork-tender.

As potatoes bake, combine cream cheese, mayonnaise, mustard, cream, salt and pepper in a small mixing bowl. Beat at medium speed with hand mixer until well blended and no lumps remain in the cheese.

Unwrap baked potatoes and cut off tops of each lengthwise, about ½ inch thick. Carefully scoop out potatoes, leaving shells intact. Place potato pulp in a large mixing bowl and mash with a potato masher.

Add cream-cheese mixture to mashed potatoes and whip with an electric mixer until smooth and well mixed. Spoon back into potato shells. Sprinkle parsley and chives on top. Arrange stuffed potatoes on a baking sheet. Heat in 350° oven for 15 minutes. Serves 6.

YAM PUDDING

- 2/3 cup sugar
- 1/3 cup light brown sugar
- 1 1/2 tsps cinnamon
- 1/2 tsp salt
- 3 eggs
- 4 Tbsps melted butter or margarine
- 1 1/2 cups milk
- 6 cups (packed) grated raw yams or sweet potatoes (see directions below before grating)
- 1/2 cup chopped pecans

Butter a large casserole and set aside. Combine sugars, cinnamon, salt, eggs, melted butter and milk in a large mixing bowl. Beat with electric mixer until well blended.

Do not grate yams until this point; otherwise they turn dark if not used immediately. Peel and grate yams and add to ingredients in the mixing bowl. Add pecans and stir well.

Turn mixture into prepared casserole. Bake in oven preheated to 325° for 1 1/4–1 1/2 hours. Serves 6.

BAKED YAMS OR SWEET POTATOES

medium-size yams or sweet potatoes
foil

Scrub yams and dry with towel. Allow 1 per person. Wrap loosely in foil, but seal tightly.

Place yams in oven preheated to 450° and bake 15 minutes. Reduce heat to 375° and cook for 1 hour. Serve with butter.

MARSHMALLOW YAMS OR SWEET POTATOES

2 to 3 lbs yams or sweet potatoes
¼ cup brown sugar
4 Tbsps butter or margarine
1 tsp cinnamon
1 Tbsp lemon juice
marshmallows

Peel yams and cut into chunks. Cover with water in a large pot and place over medium heat. Cook until well done.

Preheat oven to 400°. Drain yams. Add brown sugar, butter, cinnamon and lemon juice. Mash well with a potato masher. Mix with a spoon until ingredients are distributed evenly.

Place in a large baking dish and cover top with marshmallows. Bake in preheated oven until the top of the marshmallows are light brown. Serves 6.

SWEET POTATO PUFFS

½ cup all-purpose flour
1 tsp double-acting baking powder
½ tsp salt
½ tsp cinnamon
2½ cups cooked, mashed sweet potatoes or yams
1½ Tbsps melted butter or margarine
2 egg yolks
1 cup milk
2 Tbsps sugar
2 egg whites, stiffly beaten
oil for deep frying

Sift flour, baking powder, salt and cinnamon together. Set aside. Put mashed potatoes, melted butter, egg yolks, milk and sugar into a large mixing bowl. Beat until well mixed. Add dry ingredients and blend well.

With a large spoon, fold beaten egg whites into potato mixture carefully. Do not beat. Drop 1 tablespoon of batter at a time into hot deep fat. Cook only a few at a time to a golden brown. Drain on absorbent paper. Keep hot in warm oven until all are cooked. Serves 4 to 6.

FESTIVE MACARONI CASSEROLE

1½ cups uncooked macaroni
1 cup finely chopped fresh spinach
1 cup diced cheese
¼ cup chopped pimiento
2 Tbsps snipped chives
¼ cup chopped ripe olives
1 cup fine soft bread crumbs
4 Tbsps melted butter
1¼ cups milk
3 eggs
1 tsp Worcestershire sauce
1 tsp salt
dash nutmeg
dash cayenne pepper

Cook macaroni as directed on package until tender. Rinse in cold water and drain well. Wash spinach and towel dry before chopping. Combine cooked macaroni, spinach, cheese, pimiento, chives, olives and bread crumbs in a mixing bowl. Add melted butter and mix well.

Combine milk, eggs, Worcestershire sauce, salt and seasonings. Beat until well mixed. Turn macaroni mixture into buttered casserole. Pour sauce over macaroni. Bake in oven preheated to 350° for 40–45 minutes or until set. Serves 6.

SOUTHERN BAKED MACARONI AND CHEESE

One 12-oz package large elbow macaroni
4 Tbsps butter
4 Tbsps flour
1 tsp salt
pepper to taste
2 cups milk
1 lb Longhorn cheese, cut into small cubes

In a 6-quart pot, boil macaroni in salted water according to instructions on package until very tender. Drain in colander.

Melt butter in a saucepan. Add flour, salt and pepper. Cook and stir until smooth. Add milk ½ cup at a time, stirring vigorously. When all milk is used, cook and stir until mixture has thickened.

Remove from heat and add cheese. Stir until partially melted. Return macaroni to pot. Add cheese sauce and mix thoroughly.

Turn mixture into large buttered baking dish. Place in oven preheated to 400° and bake until bubbly and lightly browned on top. Serves 6.

CURRIED NOODLES

One 12-oz package egg noodles
3 Tbsps butter
3 Tbsps flour
1½ cups milk
1 tsp salt
1 tsp curry powder
⅛ tsp pepper
paprika

Cook noodles in boiling, slightly salted water according to directions on package. Drain thoroughly in colander.

Melt butter in a saucepan. Add flour. Stir until well blended. Slowly add milk, stirring constantly. Cook and stir over medium heat until thickened. Add salt, curry powder and pepper. Blend with a spoon.

Combine cooked noodles and sauce, stirring well. Turn into serving dish and sprinkle with paprika. Serves 6.

HERBED BUTTERED NOODLES

One 12-oz package large egg noodles
4 Tbsps butter
1 Tbsp lemon juice
3 Tbsps finely chopped green onion
3 Tbsps finely chopped parsley
3 Tbsps minced green bell pepper
One 4-oz can sliced mushrooms, drained
½ tsp seasoned salt
½ tsp coarse-ground pepper

Cook noodles in pot according to directions on package. Drain well in colander.

Melt butter in a small saucepan. Add remaining ingredients and heat thoroughly. Return noodles to pot and add butter mixture. Mix thoroughly. Turn into serving dish. Makes 6 portions.

CHEESE PUDDING

4 eggs
3 cups milk
1 Tbsp Worcestershire sauce
1 tsp seasoned salt
One 12-oz package mild Cheddar cheese, shredded

¼ cup finely chopped parsley
2 Tbsps snipped chives
5 slices bread, torn into small pieces

Preheat oven to 325°. Grease inside of a 13x9x2-inch baking dish. Set aside. Beat eggs, milk, Worcestershire sauce and salt together in a mixing bowl with an electric mixer on medium speed. Mix thoroughly.

Stir in shredded cheese, parsley and chives with a spoon. Add bread and mix well. Turn into the prepared baking dish. Bake for 45 minutes or until pudding is set. Good with steak or chops and broiled tomatoes. Serves 6.

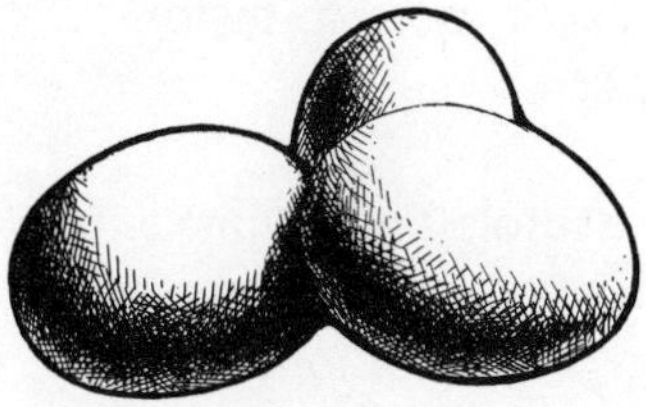

CREAMED HOMINY

Two 15-oz cans white hominy
3 Tbsps butter or margarine
3 Tbsps flour
¾ tsp salt
⅛ tsp pepper
1½ cups milk

Empty hominy into a colander and rinse with cool running water. Allow to drain.

Melt butter in a 2½-quart saucepan. Add flour, salt and pepper. Cook and stir until smooth. Pour in about ⅓ of the milk at a time, stirring vigorously. Continue until all milk is used. Cook and stir until thickened.

Add hominy. Continue to cook and stir until mixture is thoroughly hot. Turn into serving bowl. Serve as an accompaniment to meats. Makes 6 portions.

RAREBIT GRITS

5 cups cooked grits (regular, quick or instant)
¼ cup finely minced green onion
2 Tbsps finely chopped parsley
2 cups (8 ozs) shredded natural mild Cheddar cheese
¼ lb (1 stick) melted butter, cooled
1 cup light cream
3 eggs
½ cup flat beer
⅛ tsp Tabasco
1 tsp seasoned salt (or more to taste)
¼ tsp lemon pepper

Grease a large casserole and set aside. According to directions on the package, cook grits that will measure 5 cups after cooking. Remove from burner. Stir in onions, parsley, cheese and melted butter. Mix well with a spoon, cover with lid.

Combine cream, eggs, beer, Tabasco, salt and pepper in a bowl. Beat until well mixed. Stir egg mixture into grits, blending thoroughly with a spoon. Turn into prepared casserole. Bake slowly in oven preheated to 250° for 1 hour. Makes 6 to 8 servings.

HERBED RICE

½ cup finely minced green onion
¼ cup finely chopped parsley
½ tsp seasoned salt
⅛ tsp lemon pepper
½ cup water
2 cups chicken or beef broth
2 Tbsps butter or margarine
2 cups packaged precooked enriched white rice (quick)

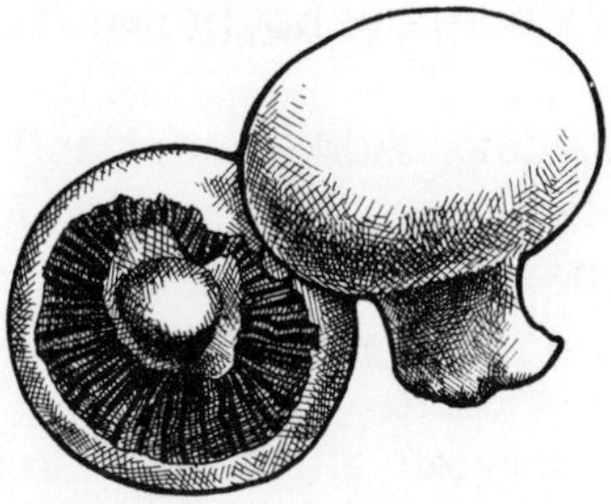

Combine onion, parsley, salt, pepper and water in a 2½-quart saucepan. Bring liquid to a boil over medium heat. Cook and stir for 1 or 2 minutes.

Add broth and butter. Bring to a rolling boil. Remove from heat and stir in rice. Cover tightly with lid and keep covered for 10–15 minutes. Fluff rice with a fork. Serve as an accompaniment to red meats, fowl or fish. Serves 6.

Note: This recipe is very basic. You may add any of the following ingredients or combination of ingredients, or you may use your own imagination: Sliced mushrooms, pimientos, chopped celery, chopped green or red bell peppers, chopped chili or Jalapeño peppers, pitted black or green olives, chopped hard-cooked eggs, or chives.

CHEESY RICE BAKE

¼ cup minced onion
¼ cup minced celery
2 Tbsps meat drippings or rendered chicken fat
1½ cups milk
1 cup shredded mild Cheddar cheese
2 eggs
4 cups cooked rice, well drained
2 Tbsps finely chopped parsley

Over low heat, sauté minced onion and celery in fat, stirring often. When onion is tender but not browned, remove from heat and set aside.

Heat milk to scalding. Add cheese and stir until melted. Remove from heat. Beat eggs with an electric mixer in a large mixing bowl. While beating, pour hot milk/cheese mixture over eggs. Blend well.

Add cooked rice, sautéed vegetables and parsley. Mix thoroughly with a spoon. Turn into a buttered casserole. Bake in oven preheated to 375° for 40–45 minutes. Serves 4 to 6.

SPANISH RICE

- 1 Tbsp cooking oil
- 2 medium ripe tomatoes, finely chopped (retain juice)
- 1 medium onion, chopped
- 1 small green bell pepper, chopped
- ½ cup sliced pitted ripe olives
- 1½ cups tomato juice
- 1 tsp chili powder
- 1 tsp salt
- ½ tsp lemon pepper
- ⅛ tsp garlic powder
- 3 cups cooked rice, well drained

Heat oil in skillet. Add chopped tomatoes, onion, green pepper and olives. Cook and stir over medium heat for 5 minutes. Add tomato juice and seasonings. Bring to a rolling boil, then turn heat to low and cover with lid. Simmer for 20 minutes.

Combine rice and sauce. Turn into buttered baking dish and bake in oven preheated to 350° until rice is the desired consistency. Serves 4 to 6.

VEGETABLES

OLD-FASHIONED GREEN BEANS

3 lbs fresh green beans
water as directed
½ lb chunk salt pork or hog jowl
salt to taste
¼ tsp pepper

Wash beans and remove strings. Snap into 2-inch lengths. Transfer beans to a Dutch oven. Wash pork thoroughly and lay chunk in center of pot. Cover beans with boiling water by 2 inches.

Bring to a rolling boil over high heat. Lower heat and cover with lid. Simmer for 2 hours and taste. Add salt if needed and pepper. Check water level occasionally. If more is needed, add boiling water.

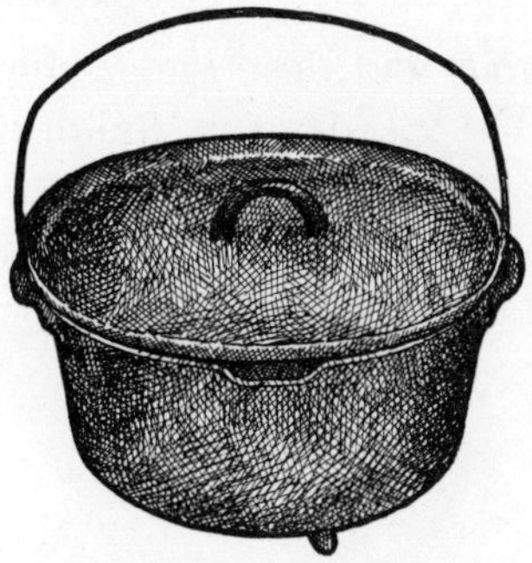

Continue to cook until beans turn a dark green. The longer they cook, the better they are. Remove lid and cook until water is low.

Great as leftovers. Serve with corn bread and new potatoes. Serves 6.

Note: Small red new potatoes may be cooked on top of the beans during the last 45 minutes of cooking time.

GREEN BEAN CASSEROLE

3	lbs fresh green beans
	water as directed
3	Tbsps dry onion soup mix
2	cans cream of chicken soup
One	8-oz can sliced water chestnuts
¼	cup fine dry bread crumbs

Wash beans and remove vine ends, tips and strings. Snap into 1-inch lengths. Rinse and place in a Dutch oven. Barely cover with slightly salted boiling water. Bring to a boil over high heat. Cover tightly and lower heat. Cook, stirring occasionally, for 45 minutes. If water cooks too low, add ½ cup water.

In a saucepan heat 1½ cups water. Add onion soup mix. Boil for 6–8 minutes. Add chicken soup, stirring constantly until smooth.

Drain beans. Drain and rinse water chestnuts. Combine the two and turn into a 13x9x2-inch baking dish. Pour soup mixture over beans. Sprinkle crumbs over top.

Bake in oven preheated to 400° for 25 minutes or until bubbly and slightly browned on top. Serves 6 to 8.

BLACK-EYED PEAS AND FRESH HAM HOCKS

2 lbs fresh ham hocks
1-lb package dried black-eyed peas
1½ tsps seasoned salt
1 Tbsp minced onion
2 Tbsps finely chopped fresh parsley
dash garlic powder
water as directed

Wash ham hocks and drop into a pot of boiling salted water. Cover and lower heat. Simmer for 1 hour.

As meat cooks, pick through peas and remove bad ones and any foreign matter. Place in colander and rinse.

Transfer ham hocks to a Dutch oven. Add rinsed peas and all other ingredients. Cover with boiling water. Bring to rolling boil. Reduce heat.

Stir and check water level occasionally, adding boiling water when needed. Do not allow mixture to stick to bottom of pot. Simmer until peas are tender and meat is done, about 1–1½ hours. Serves 6.

FRESH BLACK-EYED PEAS WITH GREEN SNAPS

4 lbs fresh black-eyed peas (see instructions below)
1 tsp lemon juice
1 tsp seasoned salt
¼ tsp pepper
dash cayenne pepper
¼ lb chunk salt pork

Select ¾ of the black-eyed peas in very full pods for shelling. Select ¼ of them very green, unfilled pods for snapping.

Shell peas and rinse. Wash snap peas well. Remove stem ends and discard. Snap peas.

Transfer peas to a pot. Cover peas with boiling water by 2 inches. Add lemon juice and seasonings.

Wash salt pork thoroughly. Place in center of pot. Place pot over high heat. Bring to a rolling boil. Reduce heat to low, cover tightly with lid. Simmer for 2½ hours. Check liquid and stir occasionally. Add more water if and when needed. Serves 6.

Fresh Black-Eyed Peas with Snaps and Okra

Follow instructions above for cooking peas. Wash 1 lb of young fresh okra well. Thirty minutes before end of cooking time, spread okra over top of peas. Re-cover tightly with lid and cook 30 minutes.

SWEET 'N' SOUR GREEN BEANS AND MUSHROOMS

3 Tbsps butter or margarine
3 small onions, sliced and divided into rings
½ cup water
¼ cup vinegar
3 Tbsps sugar
½ tsp salt
1 lb mushrooms, sliced
1 tsp cornstarch mixed with ¼ cup water
3 cups cooked or canned green beans, drained

Melt butter in a large skillet. Add onions. Cook and stir over low heat until almost tender. Add water, vinegar, sugar and salt. Stir well. Add mushrooms.

Bring mixture to a boil, then reduce heat to low. Cover with lid and simmer slowly until onions and mushrooms are tender. Add cornstarch/water mixture. Cook and stir constantly until thickened. Add green beans and mix well with a spoon. Cover and simmer for a few minutes. Serves 4 to 6.

NEW POTATOES AND GREEN PEAS

2 lbs small red new potatoes
2 lbs fresh green peas
4 Tbsps butter or margarine
4 Tbsps flour
1½ tsps salt
¼ tsp lemon pepper
2½ cups milk

Scrub potatoes and boil until tender. Drain, cool slightly and peel. Rinse and cut each in half. Set aside.

Shell peas and rinse. Cook in lightly salted boiling water until tender. Drain off liquid.

Melt butter in a saucepan. Add flour, salt and pepper. Cook and stir until smooth. Add milk a little at a time, stirring vigorously. Cook and stir until thickened.

Combine potatoes, peas and sauce in a pot. Heat thoroughly. Turn into serving bowl. Serves 6.

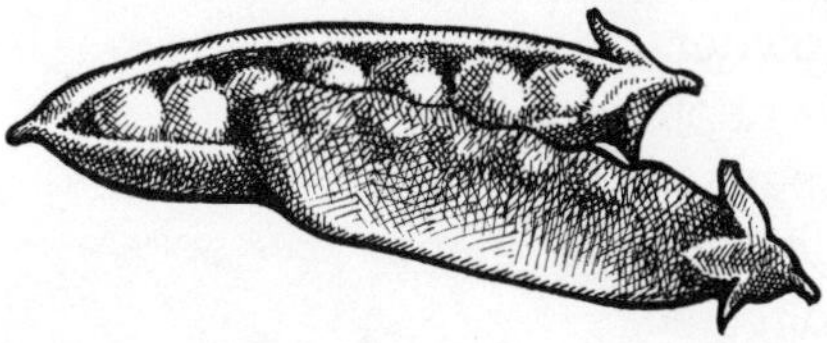

GREEN LIMAS AND MUSHROOMS

3 lbs fresh green lima beans
½ lb small white mushrooms
¼ cup sherry
1 tsp salt
¼ tsp white pepper
2 Tbsps butter
water as directed

Remove limas from shells and rinse in cool water. Wash mushrooms and cut into ¼-inch slices. Turn limas and mushrooms into a pot. Pour in enough boiling water to cover beans by about 1 inch.

Bring water to a rolling boil. Cover with lid and lower heat to medium. Allow to boil gently for 35 minutes. Add sherry, salt and pepper and stir well. Replace lid. Cook until limas are tender.

Drain most of liquid from beans. Add butter and stir. Return to burner for 2 or 3 minutes. Turn into serving bowl. Makes 6 portions.

BARBECUED BUTTER BEANS

2-lb package large dried butter beans (or large limas)
2 Tbsps dried minced onion
1 cup chopped celery and celery leaves
boiling water as directed
½ cup bottled or homemade barbecue sauce
¼ cup catsup
1 tsp liquid smoke
dash garlic powder
dash cayenne pepper
¼ tsp pepper
2 to 3 cups cubed cooked ham
salt as directed

Pick through beans and remove any bad ones and foreign matter. Rinse well and place in an 8-quart pot. Add onion and celery.

Pour enough boiling water over beans to cover them by 3 inches. Bring to a rolling boil over high heat. Turn heat to medium and cover pot with lid. If water cooks down below beans, add more boiling water to top of beans. Stir occasionally. Cook until beans are almost done.

Add barbecue sauce, catsup, liquid smoke, garlic powder, cayenne and pepper. Stir well. Return to boil and cook until beans are tender and liquid has lowered somewhat.

Add ham and stir well. Taste for salt. If needed, add desired amount.

Will serve as many as 16, but these are good left over. They may be frozen in boiling bags.

TEXAS BEAN POT

2	lbs dried pinto beans
	water as directed
½	lb salt pork
2 or 3	cloves garlic, minced
2	medium onions, chopped
One	16-oz can tomatoes
¼	cup chopped celery and leaves
3	Tbsps chili powder
1	tsp seasoned salt
½	tsp lemon pepper
1	can flat beer

Pick through beans and remove any bad ones or foreign matter. Wash beans thoroughly, then place in an 8-quart pot. Cover with boiling water plus about a 3-inch depth of water over top of beans.

Wash salt pork well. Add meat to pot either in one piece or cut into smaller pieces. Place pot over high heat until beans come to a rolling boil. Reduce heat to low, cover tightly with lid and simmer for 1 hour.

If more water is needed to keep beans covered, add boiling water so as not to disturb cooking process. At the end of 1 hour, add all remaining ingredients. Stir well.

Bring mixture back to a rolling boil, lower heat again and cover pot. Cook until beans are very tender and have made a thick gravy. Stir occasionally during cooking and add more boiling water if and when needed. Serves 6 to 8. Freeze extra in boiling bags or serve as leftovers. These beans are even better the second day.

BAKED BEANS

1 lb dried navy or white beans
water as directed
¼ cup chopped onion
¼ cup chopped celery
¼ cup chopped green bell pepper
½ cup catsup
2 Tbsps prepared mustard
½ lb salt pork or hog jowl
¼ cup molasses
¼ cup brown sugar

Pick through beans removing any bad ones and foreign matter. Wash well and rinse in a colander. Allow to drain. Place 6 cups water in a large pot. Bring to a rolling boil over high heat. Add beans, onion, celery, pepper, catsup and mustard. Stir.

Wash salt pork thoroughly. Place in center of pot with the beans. Bring mixture to a full boil, lower heat and cover with lid. Check beans occasionally and stir. If water cooks low, add boiling water as needed.

Cook until beans are tender. Remove from heat. Cut pork into small cubes and return to pot. Add molasses and sugar. Stir well.

Transfer beans to a heated Dutch oven. Place in oven preheated to 350°. Cook on lower rack until bubbly. Serves 6.

AVOCADO, CHILI BEANS AND RICE

1 lb dried pinto, pink or kidney beans
3 Tbsps cooking oil
1 large onion, chopped
2 cloves garlic, minced
1 lb lean ground beef
3 large tomatoes, peeled and sliced

1½ tsps salt
2 Tbsps chili powder
3 large ripe avocados
6 cups cooked rice

Cook beans according to instructions on the package until just fork-tender.

Heat oil in skillet. Sauté onion and garlic until onion is transparent. Add beef and crumble with spoon. Cook and stir until meat has browned. Add tomatoes, salt and chili powder. Cook and stir for 2 or 3 minutes.

Transfer meat mixture into pot with beans and mix well. Place over high heat and bring to a boil, making certain pot contains enough liquid. If not, add boiling water.

When mixture begins to boil, turn burner to low. Cover with lid and allow to simmer, stirring frequently, 20–30 minutes.

Place 1 cup hot cooked rice in each of 6 plates. Cover with ½ avocado that has been peeled and sliced. Spoon chili beans over avocado and rice. Serves 6.

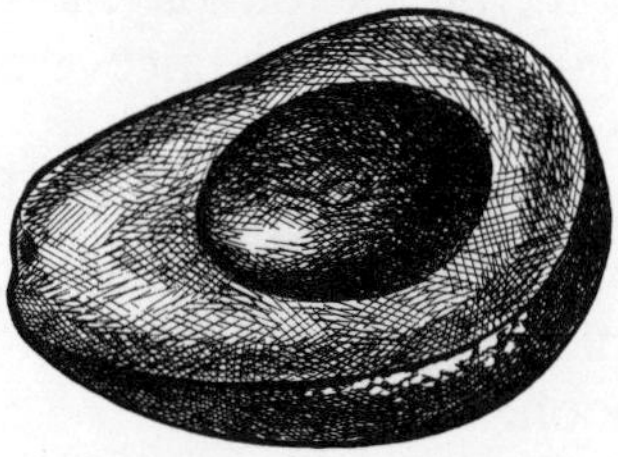

SKILLET SQUASH

2 lbs small yellow crookneck squash or small green pattypan squash
1 large onion, coarsely chopped
4 Tbsps meat drippings (or butter or margarine)
1 tsp salt
coarse-ground pepper

Scrub squash. Cut off and discard ends. Cut into slices ½ inch thick. Heat fat in heavy iron skillet. Add onion. Sauté for 2 or 3 minutes. Add squash. Stir well immediately to distribute fat and onion evenly. Place lid tightly on skillet.

Lower heat. Cook slowly and stir thoroughly occasionally. In final stage of cooking, add salt and pepper. Stir well. Cook until just tender. Serves 6.

CRUNCHY SQUASH WITH CHEESE

1 lb medium zucchini
1 lb medium yellow crookneck squash
½ lb Longhorn Cheddar cheese, coarsely shredded
One 3-oz can french-fried onions
1¼ cups slightly crushed corn chips

Scrub squash well with a vegetable brush. Cut off and discard ends. Slice all into ½-inch-thick rounds. Place in a large pot and cover with water, lightly salted. Cook uncovered over medium heat until squash is fork-tender. Drain well.

Measure and set aside ½ cup of the shredded cheese, ¼ cup of the onions and ¼ cup of the corn chips for the topping. Add remaining cheese, onions and corn chips to the drained squash, mixing well with a spoon.

Turn into buttered baking dish, sprinkle reserved ingredients over top. Bake in oven preheated to 350° for 25 minutes. Serves 4 to 6.

BAKED ACORN SQUASH

3 acorn squash
salt
pepper
melted butter

Wash squash thoroughly and dry. Cutting through stem end, slice squash into halves. Scoop seed out with a spoon. Brush melted butter liberally inside squash. Sprinkle with salt and pepper.

Place in shallow baking dish. Bake in oven preheated to 400° for 45–60 minutes or until tender and browned lightly on top. Serves 6.

BAKED BANANA SQUASH

6 pieces banana squash about 4x6 inches
melted butter
6 Tbsps brown sugar
nutmeg

Brush melted butter evenly inside squash. Sprinkle nutmeg and 1 tablespoon brown sugar over each.

Place in shallow pan in oven preheated to 350°. Bake for 45 minutes or until tender. Serves 6.

STUFFED ZUCCHINI

6 medium to large zucchini
½ lb pork sausage, cooked
1 cup herbed stuffing mix
½ cup mayonnaise
grated Parmesan cheese

Clean and cook whole zucchini in boiling salted water for about 8 minutes. Drain and slit each in half lengthwise. Scoop out centers and chop pulp into mixing bowl.

Chop cooked sausage finely and place in bowl with chopped

zucchini. Add stuffing mix and toss well. Combine mixture with mayonnaise.

Stuff zucchini shells, packing with hands and rounding the tops. Sprinkle with cheese. Place in large pan and bake in oven preheated to 350° for 30–35 minutes. Serves 6.

ZUCCHINI WITH TOMATOES AND ONIONS

4 or 5 medium zucchini
2 Tbsps butter or margarine
2 medium onions, cut into chunks
One 16-oz can tomatoes
½ tsp salt
¼ tsp Italian seasoning
water as directed
grated Parmesan cheese

Scrub zucchini with a vegetable brush. Cut into rounds about ⅓ inch thick. Set aside. Melt butter in a large skillet. Sauté onions over low heat. Cook slowly and stir for 2 to 3 minutes.

Add tomatoes, salt and seasoning. Add ½ cup water. Bring to a boil and add zucchini. Lower heat, cover tightly with lid and simmer until zucchini is tender.

Stir well and turn into serving dish. Sprinkle with Parmesan. Serves 4 to 6.

ZUCCHINI PANCAKES

1½ lbs small tender zucchini
2 tsps salt
2 eggs, beaten

¾ cup flour
¼ cup cornmeal
½ tsp lemon pepper
½ tsp onion powder
1½ Tbsps grated Parmesan cheese
3 Tbsps cooking oil

Scrub zucchini with vegetable brush. Cut off and discard ends. Grate zucchini into a large mixing bowl. Sprinkle with salt and mix well with a spoon. Cover bowl with plastic wrap and let stand for 15 minutes. Press out and pour off as much liquid as possible from bowl. Cover again and let stand another 15 minutes. Repeat pressing and draining off liquid.

Add beaten eggs to zucchini and mix well. In another bowl combine flour, cornmeal, pepper, onion powder and Parmesan. Mix with a spoon. Sprinkle a small amount of dry mixture over zucchini and mix well. Continue until all is added.

Heat oil in a skillet to sizzling. Drop heaping tablespoon of batter into hot oil. Press each down in the center with the back of the spoon as each spoonful is added to skillet. Fry pancakes a few at a time to a golden brown, turning to brown both sides. Add more oil only if needed, a small amount at a time. Drain pancakes well on absorbent paper and keep hot in warm oven until all are cooked. Serves 6.

Note: Small tender yellow or white summer squash may be substituted for the zucchini.

ASPARAGUS WITH HORSERADISH SAUCE

2½ lbs fresh green asparagus (medium-size stalks)
½ cup mayonnaise
½ cup Thousand Island dressing
1 tsp prepared mustard
1 tsp prepared horseradish
⅛ tsp lemon pepper

Wash asparagus under running water. Trim stalk ends, cutting away any tough parts. Remove small brown husks from stalks. Soak stalks in cool salted water for 30 minutes and rinse well.

Cook asparagus by steaming or boiling in lightly salted water until tender. Drain well and place lid over pot.

Combine all other ingredients in a mixing bowl. Beat with a fork until smooth. Place mixture in a small saucepan and heat (do not cook).

Arrange asparagus in serving dish. Spoon sauce over tips. If sauce seems too thick, it may be diluted by adding milk while heating in saucepan. Serves 6.

SCALLOPED CAULIFLOWER

1 large head cauliflower
5 Tbsps butter or margarine
5 Tbsps flour
1 tsp salt
3 cups milk
1 tsp coarse-ground pepper
1½ cups crumbled Saltine crackers
grated American or Parmesan cheese

Split cauliflower in quarters through the core. Cut out the core. Remove any outside leaves and any dark spots from cauliflower. Pull apart into flowerettes. Rinse under running water in colander. Place in pot. Cover with cool salted water. Allow to soak for 1 hour.

Pour off water. Cut flowerettes into uniform sizes. Cook in boiling salted water until tender. Drain and place in large casserole.

Melt butter in a saucepan. Add flour and salt. Cook and stir over medium heat until smooth. Gradually add milk, stirring vigorously. Cook and stir until thickened.

Sprinkle pepper over cauliflower and spoon sauce over it. Cover with crumbled crackers and shake cheese over top.

Place in oven preheated to 350°. Bake until bubbly and top has browned evenly. Serves 6.

BEER-BATTERED CAULIFLOWER

1 large head cauliflower
1¼ cups flat beer
3 egg yolks
1 Tbsp vegetable, peanut or olive oil
1½ cups sifted flour
3 Tbsps grated American cheese
1 tsp salt
½ tsp lemon pepper
3 egg whites

Split cauliflower head in half through core with a sharp knife. Remove core. Separate head into flowerettes. Cut larger ones to conform to size of smaller ones. Rinse well in colander. Place in container of cold salted water. Let soak for 2 hours. Drain and dry flowerettes by spreading out on a towel.

Combine beer, egg yolks and oil in mixing bowl. Add flour, cheese, salt and pepper. Beat with hand mixer until smooth and creamy.

In a separate bowl, beat egg whites until they foam and hold high peaks. Gently fold into batter.

Dip prepared flowerettes into batter and drop into deep hot fat. Do not overcrowd. Cook until golden brown. Remove and drain on absorbent paper. Continue process until all flowerettes are cooked. Serves 6.

Note: This batter may be used to coat other vegetables, as well as croquettes and seafood, for deep-frying.

CARROTS AND PEAS IN CREAM-CHEESE SAUCE

1	lb small carrots
1½	cups fresh or frozen cooked green peas
Two	3-oz packages chive cream cheese, softened at room temperature
⅔	cup light cream
½	tsp salt
½	tsp sugar
dash	lemon pepper

Peel carrots and cut into thin rounds. Cook in lightly salted water until tender. Keep carrots and cooked peas hot while preparing sauce.

Combine cream cheese, cream and seasonings in a small mixing bowl. Beat on low speed with electric mixer until smoothly mixed. Do not overbeat.

Transfer sauce to a small saucepan and heat. Do not cook. If mixture seems too thick, add a little milk. Drain liquid from carrots and peas well. Combine vegetables and sauce. Serves 6.

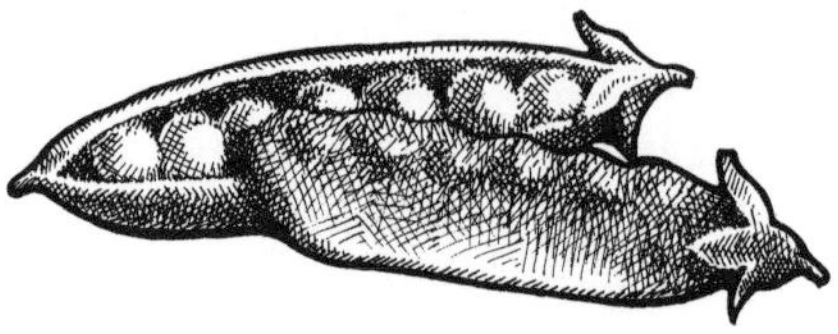

CARROTS IN SOUR CREAM

2 lbs medium fresh carrots
1 cup dairy sour cream
1 tsp salt
1 tsp sugar
3 slices crisp fried bacon, crumbled
parsley sprigs

Peel carrots and rinse in cool water. Slice into rounds ¼ inch thick. Cook in lightly salted water until tender.

In a small saucepan, combine sour cream, salt and sugar. Heat, but do not cook. Drain liquid from carrots. Add hot sour cream to carrots, stirring to coat well.

Turn into serving dish. Sprinkle with crumbled bacon and garnish with parsley. Serves 6.

WHIPPED CARROTS

2 lbs fresh carrots
3 Tbsps butter, melted
¾ cup heavy cream
¼ tsp salt
¼ tsp lemon pepper
½ tsp sugar
4 round buttered crackers, finely crushed
1 Tbsp toasted sesame seed

Peel carrots, rinse and cut into chunks. In a large pan, cover carrots with lightly salted water. Cook over medium heat until carrots are well done and can be easily mashed with a fork. Drain well and cover with lid.

Combine butter, cream, salt, lemon pepper and sugar in a

small saucepan. Heat thoroughly. Mash carrots to a pulp with a potato masher. Add cream mixture and beat with electric beater until carrots are light and fluffy.

Turn into hot serving dish. Mix cracker crumbs and toasted sesame seed and sprinkle over carrots. Serves 4 to 6.

GLAZED CARROTS

2 lbs fresh small carrots
1 cup water
1 tsp (slightly heaping) instant chicken or beef bouillon granules
1½ tsps cornstarch

Peel carrots, rinse and cover with water in a pot. Cook over medium heat until just fork-tender. Drain well and cover pot with lid.

Combine water, bouillon and cornstarch in a small saucepan. Cook and stir constantly over medium heat until thickened and bouillon has dissolved. Coat carrots with the mixture.

Drain off any excess glaze. Arrange carrots on serving dish or around meat on a large hot platter. Serves 4 to 6.

CARROT PUDDING

2 lbs fresh carrots
3 eggs
1½ cups milk
2 Tbsps softened butter or margarine
One 3-oz package pimiento cream cheese, softened at room temperature

½ tsp salt
1 Tbsp finely chopped parsley

Cook whole unpeeled carrots in boiling water until barely tender. Drain and cover with cool water, then remove the skins.

While carrots cool, combine eggs, milk, softened butter, softened cream cheese and salt. Blend until very smooth.

Coarsely grate carrots. Mix together carrots, egg/cheese mixture and parsley. Turn into buttered casserole. Bake in oven preheated to 350° for 45–50 minutes or until pudding is set. Serves 6.

BREADED CARROTS

2 lbs medium carrots (all uniform in size)
3 eggs
¾ cup cornstarch
¾ tsp salt
2 cups cracker crumbs
cooking oil

Peel carrots and leave whole. Place in a pot and cover with water. Cook over medium heat until barely tender. Drain well and spread carrots on paper towels. Allow to cool thoroughly, then slice in half lengthwise. Set aside.

Spread wax paper on a flat surface. Place small amount of crumbs in a shallow dish. Beat eggs with cornstarch and salt until well mixed. Dip one carrot half at a time in egg mixture, then coat with crumbs. Place each coated piece on the wax paper. Repeat, adding crumbs as needed to the shallow dish, until all of the carrots are coated. Pour cooking oil in an iron skillet to about ½ inch deep. Heat to sizzling.

Cook only a few carrots at a time, frying them to a golden brown on each side. Drain on absorbent paper. Keep hot in warm oven. Serves 6.

BROCCOLI SPEARS IN MUSTARD SAUCE

Two 10-oz packages frozen broccoli spears
2 eggs
½ cup white vinegar
½ cup water
3 Tbsps dry mustard
¼ cup sugar
½ tsp salt
½ tsp white pepper
2 Tbsps butter

Cook broccoli according to directions on package. Set aside and keep warm.

Combine all other ingredients except butter in a mixing bowl. Beat at medium speed until mixed thoroughly. Pour into a saucepan.

Cook and stir mixture over medium heat until it begins to boil. Add butter. Cook and stir until butter melts.

Drain broccoli well. Transfer to serving dish. Pour sauce over broccoli. Serves 6.

BROCCOLI AND RICE SCALLOP

One 16-oz package frozen chopped broccoli
1 cup milk
½ tsp seasoned salt
½ lb shredded Cheddar cheese
3 cups cooked rice
2 Tbsps butter
1 cup fine dry bread crumbs

Cook broccoli as directed on package. Drain well. Place lid on pan and set aside. Heat milk with seasoned salt. Add cheese and stir until melted. Combine cooked broccoli, cooked rice and cheese mixture, blending with a spoon.

Turn into a large buttered baking dish. Melt butter and mix with bread crumbs. Sprinkle buttered crumbs over broccoli mixture. Bake in oven preheated to 350° until bubbly and lightly browned on top. Serves 6.

BROCCOLI IN LEMON BUTTER

2 bunches fresh broccoli (or two 10-oz packages frozen broccoli spears)
¼ cup fine dry bread crumbs
3 Tbsps grated Romano cheese
⅓ cup melted butter
3 Tbsps lemon juice

Choose evenly green fresh broccoli with small closed buds. Trim stems and stem ends. Rinse under cool running water. Cut into spears and cover with cool salted water. Soak for 30 minutes. Drain and rinse.

Steam fresh or frozen broccoli or cook in lightly salted boiling water until tender.

Lightly brown crumbs in a small shallow pan in oven. Mix with cheese and set aside. Heat butter and skim off foam with a spoon. Mix butter and lemon juice.

Drain water from broccoli and arrange vegetable in serving dish. Drizzle lemon butter over top and sprinkle with cheesy crumbs. Serves 6.

ROASTED CORN

6 ears tender sweet corn
melted butter
seasoned salt
lemon pepper
shucks from corn

Discard only outer shucks from corn. Save all of the others. Rinse shucks well under running water. Place half of shucks in the bottom of a roaster. Remove all silks from corn and cut off cob end even with kernels.

Brush ears with melted butter. Sprinkle with seasoned salt and lemon pepper. Place on top of shucks in roaster. Cover with remaining shucks. Place lid tightly on roaster.

Place in oven preheated to 400°. Bake for 45 minutes or until corn is tender. Serves 6.

CORN FRITTERS

⅔ cup all-purpose flour
¾ tsp soda
½ tsp salt
⅔ cup buttermilk

2 eggs
2 cups canned cut whole-kernel corn, drained
oil for frying

Measure, then sift flour, soda and salt together. Beat buttermilk and eggs together well. Combine with flour mixture and whip until smooth. Add drained corn and mix thoroughly.

Pour oil ½ inch deep in an iron skillet. Heat to sizzling. Using about ¼ cup of batter for each fritter, fry a few fritters at a time to a light golden brown on each side. Drain on absorbent paper. Keep hot in warm oven. Serve hot. Makes about 18 fritters.

FRIED FRESH CORN

3 slices bacon
4 cups fresh sweet corn, cut and scraped from cobs
2 tsps sugar
⅛ tsp white pepper
1 cup milk
1 Tbsp cornstarch
salt if needed

In an iron skillet, fry bacon over medium heat to almost the crisp stage. Add corn, sugar and pepper to the bacon and drippings. Stir vigorously to mix.

Cook and stir for 4 or 5 minutes, browning the corn slightly. Mix cornstarch with milk thoroughly. Pour mixture over corn, stirring constantly. Cook and stir over medium heat until thickened. If too thick, add more milk. Taste and add salt if needed. Serves 6.

ONIONS IN CREAM SAUCE

1½ lbs small whole boiling onions, peeled
4 Tbsps butter or margarine
4 Tbsps flour
1 tsp salt
½ tsp sugar
⅛ tsp white pepper
2 cups milk

Plunge onions into a pot of lightly salted boiling water. Cook until onions are barely tender. Drain, return to pot, and keep warm.

Melt butter in a saucepan over medium heat. Add flour. Cook and stir until smooth. Add salt, sugar, pepper and ½ cup milk. Stir vigorously. Add remaining milk. Cook and stir until sauce has thickened and no lumps remain.

Pour sauce over onions and mix with a spoon. Transfer to a serving bowl. Serves 6.

FRIED ONION RINGS

3 or 4 large onions
oil for frying
2 eggs
1 tsp salt
1 Tbsp peanut oil
1 cup flour
3 Tbsps cornmeal
¾ cup milk

Peel onions and slice ¼ inch thick. Separate into rings. Pour oil into a deep fryer to about 2 inches deep. While oil heats, beat eggs, salt and peanut oil together, then alternately add flour, cornmeal and milk. Beat to a smooth batter.

Pick out the larger rings first. When oil is hot, but not smoking, dip rings into the batter one at a time and drop into the hot oil. Fry only a few at a time.

Remove each batch of cooked rings to absorbent paper and keep hot in oven until all are cooked. Serve hot. Enough for 6.

HERBED BUTTERED LEEKS

2 bunches (about 1 lb each) leeks
6 Tbsps butter
2 Tbsps finely chopped parsley
⅛ tsp seasoned salt
⅛ tsp lemon pepper
1 tsp prepared mustard
¼ cup fine dry bread crumbs, toasted to a light brown

Cut off root ends of leeks. Trim tops to a point by making diagonal slits from each side to center. Remove all coarse outer leaves leaving tender inner ones. Split each leek in half to within ½ inch of end. Under running water gently separate leaves and rinse away dirt between them.

Divide leeks into 4 bunches and tie both ends of each bunch with cord. Place in a large pot. Pour 1 quart of boiling salted water over leeks. Place over high heat and bring to a boil. Reduce heat and cook until tender, 15–20 minutes.

Remove leeks gently from water and drain. Snip off cords. Place in serving dish. Keep warm while making topping.

Melt butter in saucepan. Add parsley, seasoned salt, pepper and mustard. Stir until butter melts and is bubbly. Remove pan from burner and stir in toasted crumbs. Mix well. Spoon mixture over leeks. Serves 6.

BEETS IN ORANGE SAUCE

Two 16-oz cans whole baby beets
⅓ cup frozen orange juice concentrate (undiluted)
1½ Tbsps cornstarch mixed with ¼ cup water

Drain juice from beets into a saucepan. Add orange juice. Cook over high heat to boiling. Add cornstarch mixture and stir vigorously. Cook until thickened.

Add beets. Turn heat to medium. Cook only until beets are hot. Serves 6.

FRESH BUTTERED BEETS

9 to 12 medium-size fresh beets
boiling water as directed
2 Tbsps vinegar or lemon juice
4 Tbsps salted butter, melted

Choose clean, smooth beets. Cut off top, leaving 1 inch of stem above beets, and leave on root end. Wash thoroughly.

Place in a large pot. Cover beets with boiling water by 1 inch. Add vinegar or lemon juice.

Boil over medium heat for 1 hour or until beets are tender (old beets will never be tender). Add boiling water if needed while cooking.

When beets are done, drain off water. Allow to cool enough to handle. Peel and stem. Cut into slices ¼ inch thick and place in mixing bowl. Pour butter over beets. Mix until all slices are coated. Transfer to serving dish. Serves 6.

Note: You may use two 16-oz cans sliced beets. Heat beets in their own juice, drain and add butter as directed above.

BEETS IN CREAM

4 cups (hot) sliced cooked fresh or canned beets, well drained
¾ cups dairy sour cream
3 Tbsps beet juice or milk
½ tsp salt (or more to taste)
1 tsp sugar
2 tsps prepared horseradish
dash cayenne pepper

See preceding recipe for cooking beets. Combine all ingredients except beets in a saucepan. Place over medium heat and stir until sauce is very hot. Do not boil. Mix sauce with hot beets, coating each slice. Makes 6 servings.

FRIED OKRA

2 lbs bright green fresh okra
salt
pepper
¾ cup cornmeal
⅓ cup cooking oil
water as directed

Wash okra thoroughly. Cut off stem ends of pods. Slice okra into rounds about ½ inch thick and place in a large mixing bowl.

Salt and pepper the okra and mix in with hands. Add cornmeal and mix well.

Heat oil over high heat in a very large iron skillet. Tilt pan and allow oil to spread up sides of skillet. Heat until a drop of water sizzles and pops when added to oil.

With both hands remove some of the okra, shaking off any loose meal, and place it in skillet. Continue until all is in skillet. Immediately stir well to distribute oil.

Turn heat to medium and cover tightly with lid. Stir often and cook until okra is evenly browned. Pour about ¼ cup of water over okra and cover immediately. Allow to cook until steaming stops. Stir well. Serves 6.

OKRA GUMBO

- 2 Tbsps olive oil or meat drippings
- 1 lb fresh or frozen okra, cut into ½-inch rounds
- 3 medium red ripe tomatoes, peeled and cut into pieces
- 1 large onion, chopped coarsely
- 2 cups fresh, frozen or canned whole-kernel corn, drained
- 1 tsp salt (or more to taste)
- ¼ tsp pepper
- 1 Tbsp wine vinegar
- 1 cup water (or more when needed)

Heat oil in a large skillet. Sauté okra, tomatoes, onion and corn, stirring constantly for 10 minutes. Combine salt, pepper, vinegar and water. Pour over vegetables.

Bring to a boil, then turn to low heat. Cover and let simmer. Stir occasionally, adding ½ cup boiling water at a time, as it is needed. Cook until vegetables are tender, about 30 minutes. Serves 4 to 6.

CHILI RELLENOS

8 to 12	large green chili peppers (allow 2 per person)
2	cups shredded Monterey Jack cheese
	flour for dredging
4	egg yolks, beaten
½	cup heavy cream
½	tsp salt
⅓	cup all-purpose flour
4	egg whites, stiffly beaten
	light vegetable oil, as directed

Salsa:

Two	16-oz cans tomatoes
1	large onion, chopped
2	Tbsps vinegar
2	tsps sugar
¼	tsp salt
½	tsp chili powder
dash	garlic salt
dash	cayenne pepper

Make Salsa first. Drain juice from tomatoes into a large saucepan. Chop tomatoes and add to pan along with all other sauce ingredients. Bring to a boil over medium heat. Reduce heat to low, cover with lid and simmer until onion is tender. Remove from heat and set aside.

In order to remove skins from peppers, place them under the broiler. Turn as needed so they will broil until blistered all over. They may turn black, which is all right. Remove and, while peppers are still very hot, wrap them tightly in foil so they may "sweat" for a few minutes. Unwrap and remove and discard skins.

Make a slit on one side of each pepper. Remove stems and seeds. Stuff peppers with shredded cheese, then roll in flour. Set aside.

Make a batter by beating egg yolks, cream, salt and ⅓ cup of flour together in a mixing bowl. Beat until smooth. Carefully fold in stiffly beaten egg whites. Pour oil ½ inch deep into a heavy skillet. Heat until sizzling.

One at a time, dip peppers into batter and place in the hot oil. Cook only 2 or 3 at a time. When brown on bottom, turn and brown other side. Drain on absorbent paper. Keep hot in warm oven until all are cooked. Reheat sauce and serve with peppers. Serves 4 to 6.

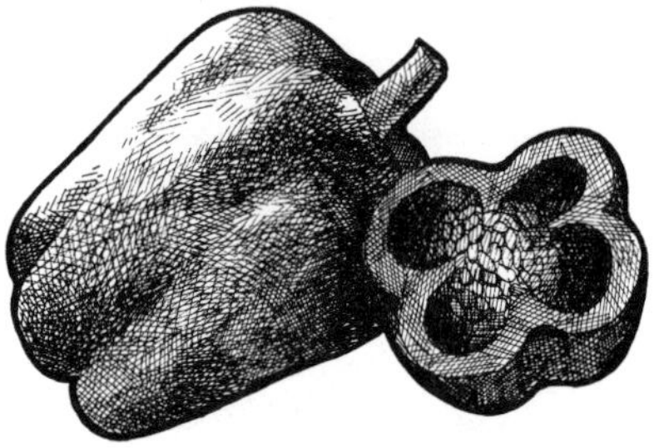

EGGPLANT CASSEROLE

2 medium eggplants
1½ tsps salt
½ tsp pepper
½ tsp rubbed sage
cooking oil as directed
One 8-oz package corn bread stuffing mix
One 4-oz jar chopped pimiento
1¾ cups milk
1 cup sliced celery
⅔ cup chopped onion
⅓ cup chopped green bell pepper
2 eggs, beaten
¼ lb (1 stick) butter or margarine, melted
⅓ cup grated Parmesan cheese

Wash eggplants and remove and discard stem ends. Cut into 1-inch cubes. Heat 3 tablespoons cooking oil in a Dutch oven. Add eggplant, salt, pepper and sage. Stir to distribute seasonings evenly.

Cook, stirring occasionally, over medium heat until eggplant is tender.

Combine stuffing mix, pimiento and milk in a bowl. Stir well, then allow to soak. Heat 2 tablespoons oil in a small skillet. Sauté celery, onion and green pepper until limp.

Stir beaten eggs and melted butter into stuffing mixture. Combine all ingredients with eggplant. Mix well. Turn into greased 13x9x2-inch Pyrex dish. Sprinkle cheese over top.

Bake in oven preheated to 350° for 40 minutes. Serves 6.

FRIED GREEN TOMATOES

- 6 medium firm green tomatoes
- ½ cup cooking oil
- ¾ cup yellow cornmeal
- ¼ cup all-purpose flour
- 1½ tsps salt
- ½ tsp pepper
- 1 egg
- ½ cup milk

Wash tomatoes and remove the outer part of core. Do not peel. Slice ½ inch thick. Spread out on paper towels to drain.

Heat oil in a large heavy iron skillet to sizzling, but do not let it smoke. As oil heats, make batter.

Combine cornmeal, flour, salt, pepper, egg and milk. Beat until well mixed. Dip tomato slices into batter and drop in skillet. Do not overcrowd. Brown quickly, turning once. Drain on absorbent paper. Keep warm in oven until serving. Makes 6 portions.

BROILED TOMATOES

6 medium to large tomatoes (allow 1 per person)
¼ lb melted butter or margarine
½ tsp seasoned salt
½ tsp lemon pepper
⅛ tsp onion powder
cracker meal

Cut off and discard tops and bottoms of tomatoes. Slice each tomato in half horizontally. Combine melted butter and seasonings. Mix well.

Dip tomato halves in butter mixture, then coat with cracker meal. Place on baking sheet and place under broiler. Cook until lightly browned. Carefully turn and broil other sides. Serves 6.

SCALLOPED TOMATOES

Two 16-oz cans stewed tomatoes
2 Tbsps melted butter or margarine
3 Tbsps sugar
¼ tsp salt
4 slices white bread
shredded cheese (optional)

Empty tomatoes into a mixing bowl. Cut into smaller pieces. Add butter, sugar and salt. Stir well.

Pull bread apart into small pieces. Mix with tomatoes. Turn into a buttered casserole.

Bake in oven preheated to 350° for 45 minutes. Cheese may be sprinkled over top during last minutes of cooking. Serves 6.

RUTABAGAS WITH SALT PORK

2 to 3 lbs rutabagas
water as directed
1 Tbsp sugar
¼ tsp pepper
½-lb chunk salt pork

Peel rutabagas and rinse. Cut into ½-inch cubes and place in a Dutch oven. Cover with water and sprinkle with sugar and pepper. Wash salt pork thoroughly to remove salt and place in center of pot.

Bring to a rolling boil. Cover with lid and reduce heat. Simmer, stirring occasionally. (The longer the rutabaga cooks, the better it is.) Cook until meat and rutabaga are very tender. Serves 6 to 8.

MASHED TURNIPS

2 lbs small purple-top turnips, peeled and cut into chunks
2 Tbsps butter
1 tsp salt
1 Tbsp sugar
½ tsp lemon pepper
paprika

Barely cover turnips with water in a pot. Cover pot and cook turnips until very tender. Drain in a colander. Return turnips to pot and mash well with a potato masher.

Add all other ingredients to pot and stir well. Place over medium heat. Cook and stir until the mixture is the consistency of mashed potatoes. Turn into a serving dish and sprinkle lightly with paprika. Serves 4 to 6.

TURNIP GREENS WITH TURNIPS

3 bunches turnips with young green tops
½ lb salt pork
3 cups water
salt to taste

Cut turnips from tops and peel. Set aside. Remove any tough stem ends from leaves and remove any discolored leaves. Wash each leaf separately under running water. Allow to drain.

Wash salt pork thoroughly, removing all salt. Cut meat into ¼-inch-thick slices. Place in a 6-quart pot with the water. Bring to a rolling boil over high heat. Add greens and return to boiling. Stir until greens have wilted down somewhat.

Cover with lid and turn burner to medium. Cook 45 minutes, checking liquid. If more is needed, add boiling water.

Cut turnips into large chunks. Place on top of greens. Return to boil. Taste liquid. If salt is needed, sprinkle in desired amount. Check liquid level occasionally. Cook until turnips are very tender.

Great with sliced tomatoes, green onions and corn bread. Serves 6.

BOILED CABBAGE

1 large head green cabbage
3 cups water
1 tsp salt (or more to taste)
pepper to taste
3 Tbsps meat drippings or butter

Remove and discard outer leaves of cabbage. Split cabbage into quarters, starting at stem end. Remove core from all four pieces. Cut cabbage into chunks about 1½ inches square. Place in colander and rinse with cool running water.

Pour water and salt into a large pot. Bring to a rolling boil over high heat. Add prepared cabbage. Bring back to boil. Set heat to medium and cover pot with lid.

Cook, stirring occasionally, for 25 minutes. Add pepper and fat. Stir to mix. Cook an additional 10 minutes. Turn into serving bowl. Serves 6.

SWEET AND SOUR CABBAGE

1 medium head green cabbage
4 Tbsps butter or margarine
⅔ cup pineapple juice
3 Tbsps wine vinegar
2 Tbsps sugar
¾ tsp salt
⅛ tsp dillweed
½ cup water

Discard outer leaves of cabbage and core it. Cut cabbage into thin strips. Combine all other ingredients in a large pot. Heat until butter is melted and mixture comes to a boil. Add cabbage and stir well to coat with liquid.

Cover with lid and cook over medium heat, stirring thoroughly occasionally. Cook until cabbage is very tender. Add more water if needed during cooking. Drain off liquid and turn into serving dish. Serves 6.

BAKED SPINACH AND RICE

3 eggs
1 cup milk
2 Tbsps snipped chives
2 tsps Worcestershire sauce
1 tsp salt
dash garlic powder
dash Tabasco
3 cups cooked and drained chopped spinach
2 cups cooked rice
4 Tbsps melted butter
2 cups shredded sharp Cheddar cheese

Combine eggs, milk, chives, Worcestershire sauce, salt, garlic powder and Tabasco in a large mixing bowl. Beat until well mixed and frothy. Add cooked spinach, rice, butter and 1¼ cups of the cheese. Mix well with a spoon.

Turn into a buttered baking dish and place in oven preheated to 350°. Bake for 45 minutes. Remove and sprinkle remaining ¾ cup cheese over top. Return to oven for 10 minutes. Serves 6.

WILTED LETTUCE

2 heads fresh leaf lettuce
3 slices bacon
3 Tbsps vinegar
½ tsp salt
dash pepper
2 green onions, chopped

Remove stems from heads of lettuce. Wash leaves well and drain in a colander.

Fry bacon in a large iron skillet. Remove bacon, crumble and set aside.

Add vinegar, salt and pepper to the bacon drippings in skillet. Mix with spoon. Heat mixture to bubbling. Add lettuce and chopped green onions. Toss well while heating until lettuce wilts. Garnish with crumbled bacon. Makes 4 to 6 portions.

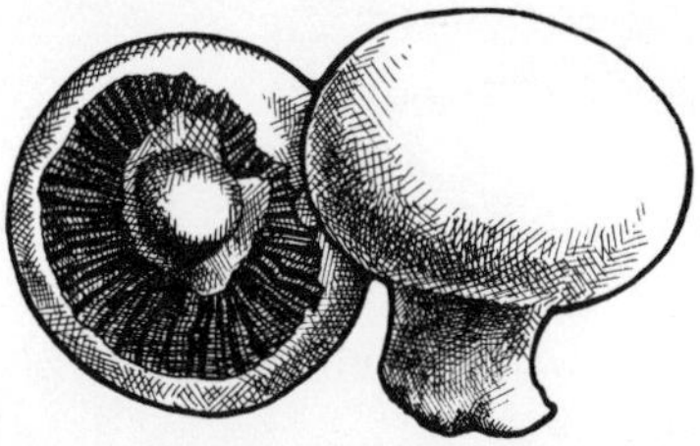

HASHED BRUSSELS SPROUTS

- 1½ lbs fresh Brussels sprouts (see note)
- 2 Tbsps peanut oil
- ½ cup water
- ½ tsp salt
- ⅛ tsp lemon pepper
- dash hot pepper sauce
- One 4-oz can sliced mushrooms, drained
- Parmesan cheese

Remove any bad outer leaves and excessive stems from sprouts. Soak in cool water for one hour. Drain and rinse well. Slice each sprout into 3 or 4 pieces.

Place oil in a medium-size skillet over moderate heat. When hot, add sprouts and stir-fry for 3 or 4 minutes. Mix together water, salt, pepper, and pepper sauce. Stir well then pour over sprouts. Cover and cook for 5 to 6 minutes, stirring once.

Add mushrooms and mix. Cover and cook for about 2 more minutes. Spoon mixture into serving dish. Sprinkle Parmesan on top. Serves 4 to 6.

Note: Two 10-oz packages of frozen Brussels sprouts may be substituted for the fresh ones. Allow to thaw at room temperature before slicing.

DESSERTS

OLD-FASHIONED JAM CAKE

2 cups all-purpose flour
½ tsp salt
1 tsp baking soda
1 tsp double-acting baking powder
¾ cup sugar
¾ cup vegetable oil
1 cup buttermilk
3 eggs, well beaten
1 tsp rum or brandy flavoring
1 cup raspberry, boysenberry, mulberry or blackberry jam (see note below)
1 cup chopped nuts mixed with 1 Tbsp flour

Glaze:

1½ cups sifted powdered sugar
3½ Tbsps hot water
1 tsp lemon juice
2 tsps white corn syrup

Preheat oven to 325°. Grease and flour a 13x9x2-inch Pyrex baking dish.

Sift flour, salt, soda and baking powder together. Set aside. Combine sugar, oil, buttermilk, eggs and flavoring in a large mixing bowl. Beat until well mixed.

Gradually add sifted dry ingredients to buttermilk mixture,

beating until thoroughly blended. Add jam (see note below) and nuts. Stir until mixed thoroughly.

Turn into prepared baking dish. Bake in oven preheated to 325° for 45 minutes. Allow to cool in pan for 15 minutes, then make glaze.

To make glaze:

Combine all ingredients in a saucepan. Stir until mixed thoroughly. Heat for a few seconds over medium heat, stirring constantly. Drizzle glaze over cake. Allow to cool for 2 hours.

Note: If jam is not seedless, I prefer, especially for blackberry, to press it through a strainer and remove seeds. If you remove seeds, add ¼ cup more jam to this recipe.

APRICOT SNACKING CAKE

One	6-oz package dried apricots
3	cups all-purpose flour
1	tsp baking soda
1	tsp salt
1½	cups vegetable or peanut oil
3	eggs
1	tsp brandy flavoring
2	cups sugar
1	Tbsp lemon juice
1	cup chopped nuts (preferably pecans or walnuts)

Glaze:

1½ cups sifted powdered sugar
4 Tbsps apricot nectar
1 tsp lemon juice

Cover apricots with water and soak for 2 or 3 hours. Drain and towel dry. Chop fruit finely. Set aside. Sift premeasured flour, soda and salt together. Set aside.

In a mixing bowl, combine oil, eggs, flavoring, sugar and lemon juice. Stir and beat until well mixed. Adding about ⅓ of the dry ingredients at a time, blend well with a spoon. Continue to add dry ingredients and mix until batter is smooth. Fold in chopped apricots and nuts until thoroughly blended.

Grease and flour inside of a 13x9x2-inch baking dish. Turn batter into dish. Bake in oven preheated to 325° for 1 hour or until wooden toothpick inserted in center of cake comes out clean. Allow cake to cool.

Apricot glaze:

Beat together powdered sugar, apricot nectar and lemon juice until well blended. Drizzle over top of cake.

Cut cake into squares and serve directly from baking dish.

DATE NUT CAKE

¾ cup vegetable shortening
1½ cups (firmly packed) brown sugar
1 lb pitted dates, chopped
2 cups chopped pecans
1 cup boiling water
2 Tbsps whiskey or brandy
3 eggs, well beaten
2¼ cups all-purpose flour
1 tsp baking soda
¾ tsp salt

Glaze:

1 cup powdered sugar
3 tsps water
1 tsp whiskey or brandy

Cream shortening and sugar in a large mixing bowl and beat until fluffy. Add dates and pecans. Pour boiling water and whiskey over mixture and blend well with a spoon. Add beaten eggs and mix.

Sift flour, soda and salt together and mix with date mixture, beating until smooth.

Turn into a greased and floured 13x9x2-inch pan. Bake in oven preheated to 300° for 1½ hours.

To make glaze:

Combine powdered sugar, water and whiskey or brandy and beat until smooth. If too thick, add a small amount of water. Drizzle over cake while it is still warm.

BEST-IN-THE-WORLD CHEESECAKE

Bottom:

1¼ cups fine graham cracker crumbs
3 Tbsps sugar
5½ Tbsps butter or margarine

Grease inside of an 8x8x2-inch Pyrex dish or a springform pan. Combine crumbs and sugar in a small mixing bowl. Melt butter slowly in a small saucepan, taking care not to burn it. Pour butter over crumb mixture and blend well with a fork. Press mixture onto bottom of prepared pan, packing firmly with hands. Set aside.

Cake:

Two 8-oz packages cream cheese, softened to room temperature
½ cup milk
⅔ cup sugar
3 eggs
⅛ tsp salt
1 tsp vanilla
3 Tbsps lemon juice

Preheat oven to 350°. Place softened cheese and all other ingredients in a mixing bowl. Beat with electric mixer until creamy and smooth. Make certain no lumps remain. Pour batter over graham cracker bottom in prepared pan. Bake in preheated oven for 40–45 minutes. Remove from oven and allow to cool for 20–25 minutes (this is important).

Topping:

½ pt (1 cup) dairy sour cream
3 Tbsps sugar
½ tsp vanilla

Stir all ingredients together, mixing well. After cake has cooled for 20–25 minutes, spread topping on cake and return to preheated oven for 10 minutes. Remove from oven and cool. Refrigerate for at least 4 hours or preferably overnight before serving.

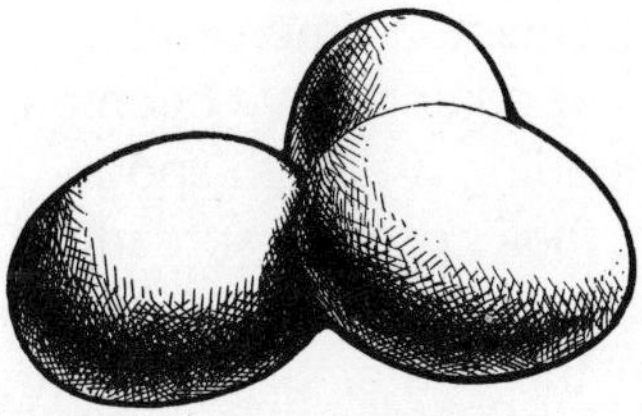

PEAR SNACKING CAKE

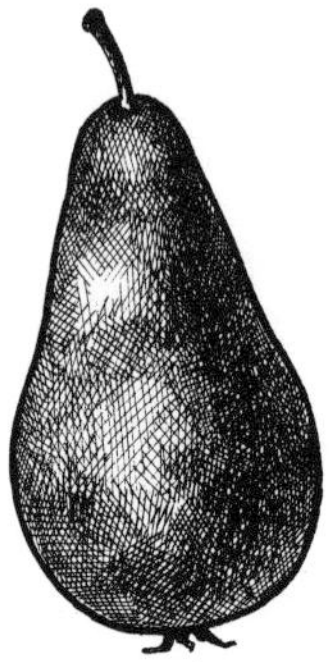

- 3 cups all-purpose flour
- 1 tsp baking soda
- 1 tsp salt
- ¼ tsp nutmeg
- ¼ tsp ginger
- 1½ tsps cinnamon
- 1 cup sugar
- 1 cup (packed) light brown sugar
- 3 eggs
- 1½ cups vegetable oil
- 1 tsp vanilla
- ½ tsp brandy flavoring
- 3 cups coarsely diced canned or fresh pears*
- ½ cup chopped nuts (preferably pecans or walnuts)

Glaze:

- 1½ cups sifted powdered sugar
- ¼ cup warm milk
- ¼ tsp vanilla

Preheat oven to 325°. Grease and flour the inside of a 13x9x2-inch baking dish. Set aside. Sift together flour, soda, salt and spices. Set aside.

In a large mixing bowl, combine sugars, eggs, oil and flavorings. Beat with hand mixer until well blended. Add about ¾ cup of the dry ingredients at a time, beating with spoon after each addition until all dry ingredients have been thoroughly mixed. Fold in pears and nuts, blending well with spoon.

Turn batter into baking dish, spreading evenly on top with back of spoon. Bake in preheated oven for 1 hour or until wooden toothpick inserted in the center of cake comes out clean. Allow cake to cool in dish.

To make glaze:

Combine sifted powdered sugar, warm milk and vanilla and beat until smooth. Drizzle glaze over top of cake.

Cut cake into squares and serve directly from baking dish.

*When using canned pears, drain thoroughly, then blot each pear half with paper towels. Coarsely dice enough for 3 cups. If using fresh pears, choose ripe ones. Peel and core. Dice pears to measure 3 cups.

MOCHA NUT CAKE

- ¾ cup vegetable shortening
- 2 cups sugar
- 3 cups sifted cake flour
- ¼ tsp salt
- 2 tsps double-acting baking powder
- 3 Tbsps cocoa
- 2 tsps instant coffee
- 1 cup milk
- 1 tsp vanilla
- 5 egg whites

Mocha Nut Frosting:

- ⅓ cup butter
- 2 Tbsps milk
- 2 Tbsps cocoa
- 1 tsp instant coffee
- 1 1-lb box powdered sugar
- 1 tsp vanilla
- ½ cup finely chopped nuts

Combine shortening and sugar in a large mixing bowl. Cream together with a spoon, then beat until fluffy.

Sift together flour, salt, baking powder, cocoa and coffee. Alternately add flour mixture and milk to shortening and sugar, mixing well.

Stir in vanilla. Beat egg whites until stiff and fold them carefully into cake batter.

Turn into two greased and floured 9-inch-round cake pans. Bake in oven preheated to 350° for 25–30 minutes or until wooden toothpick inserted in center comes out clean. Cool cakes in pans for 10 minutes; turn out on rack to cool completely.

To make frosting:

Melt butter over low heat in a saucepan. Add milk, cocoa and coffee. Mix well with spoon. Sift powdered sugar and add slowly to butter mixture, stirring vigorously. Stir in vanilla and nuts. If mixture seems too thick, add small amount of hot milk until frosting is of spreading consistency.

Place 1 cake layer on plate and spread top with frosting. Add second layer and spread frosting on top and sides of cake.

APPLESAUCE CAKE

3¼ cups sifted flour (save ¼ cup to mix with nuts)
2 tsps cinnamon
¼ tsp cloves
⅛ tsp allspice
⅛ tsp nutmeg
2 tsps baking soda
½ tsp salt
¼ lb (1 stick) butter, softened
½ cup vegetable shortening
2 cups sugar
2 large eggs
2 cups sweetened applesauce
2 cups chopped nuts (pecans preferred)
1½ cups seedless raisins
½ cup chopped candied pineapple

Sift flour, spices, soda and salt together. Set aside.

Combine butter and shortening in a large mixing bowl. With a hand mixer, cream together until fluffy. Gradually add sugar, beating well. Beat in eggs one at a time. Add applesauce and dry ingredients a little at a time, mixing until all have been added.

In another bowl, mix nuts, raisins and pineapple with ¼ cup flour until ingredients are coated. Fold the mixture into the cake batter. Grease and flour a 9-inch tube pan. Spoon batter into pan and spread evenly.

Bake in oven preheated to 350° for 1¼–1½ hours or until cake pulls away from sides of pan. Cool in pan for 25 minutes. Turn out on a wire rack. Dribble a light glaze over top if desired. Do not cut for 3 hours.

SUNSHINE CAKE

2½ cups all-purpose flour
3 tsps double-acting baking powder
½ tsp baking soda
1 tsp salt
1½ cups sugar
⅔ cup vegetable shortening
3 eggs
¾ cup milk
¼ cup defrosted orange juice concentrate, undiluted
1 cup flaked coconut
1 cup coarsely chopped white raisins

Topping:

One 3-oz package cream cheese, softened to room temperature
3 Tbsps defrosted orange juice concentrate, undiluted
2 tsps water
1 cup whipping cream

Grease well the inside of a 13x9x2-inch baking dish. Set aside. Sift flour, baking powder, soda and salt together and set aside.

In a large mixing bowl, combine sugar and shortening. Cream well with a spoon. Add eggs and milk. Beat until just mixed. Add ½ of the flour mixture and mix with spoon. Add remaining dry ingredients and orange juice concentrate. At medium speed, beat with electric mixer for 3 minutes, scraping bowl and blades as needed.

Add flaked coconut and chopped raisins. Stir with a spoon until ingredients are distributed evenly. Turn into the prepared baking dish and spread top evenly with a spoon. Bake in oven preheated to 350° for 35–40 minutes or until done.

To make topping:

Combine softened cheese, juice concentrate and water in a bowl. Beat at medium speed with electric mixer until blended. Add cream and beat until mixture will hold peaks. Cut cake into squares. Swirl whipped topping on each square.

PRUNE CAKE SUPREME

- 2 cups all-purpose flour
- ½ tsp salt
- 1½ tsps baking soda
- 1 tsp cinnamon
- 1 tsp allspice
- ½ tsp nutmeg
- 1½ cups (packed) light brown sugar
- 1 cup vegetable oil
- 1 cup buttermilk
- 3 eggs, well beaten
- 1 tsp vanilla
- 1 tsp rum or brandy flavoring
- 1 cup cooked pitted prunes, cut up
- 1 cup chopped nuts
- ½ cup chopped candied pineapple (optional)

Topping:

1 cup sugar
½ cup buttermilk
½ tsp baking soda
1 Tbsp corn syrup
4 Tbsps butter
½ tsp rum or brandy flavoring

Grease and flour inside of a 13x9x2-inch baking dish. Sift together flour, salt, soda and spices into a large mixing bowl. Stir in sugar. Add oil, buttermilk, beaten eggs and flavorings. Mix thoroughly. Stir in prunes, nuts and pineapple, mixing well.

Bake in prepared pan in oven preheated to 325° for 45 minutes. Make topping immediately after removing cake from oven.

To make topping:

Combine sugar, buttermilk, soda and syrup in a saucepan. Add butter. Place over medium heat and bring to a boil. Cook for just 1 minute after boiling starts. Stir in flavoring. Pour hot over warm cake. Cool for 3 or 4 hours before cutting.

RUM CAKE

One 18½-oz package yellow cake mix
One 3½-oz package vanilla instant pudding and pie mix
¼ cup poppy seed
⅛ tsp allspice
¼ tsp cinnamon
½ cup peanut or vegetable oil
4 eggs
¼ cup light rum
½ cup milk

Glaze:

1½ cups sifted powdered sugar
1 Tbsp light rum
¼ cup hot water

Grease and flour well inside of a Bundt pan. Set aside. Combine the mixes, poppy seed and spices in a large mixing bowl. Blend well with a spoon.

Add oil, eggs, rum and milk. Beat with electric mixer on medium speed for 3 or 4 minutes. Turn batter into prepared pan. Bake in oven preheated to 350° for 35–40 minutes or until wooden toothpick inserted in center of cake comes out clean. Cool for 30 minutes in pan. Turn out of pan.

To make glaze:

Mix together powdered sugar, rum and hot water and beat with a spoon until smooth. Drizzle warm glaze over Rum Cake.

ORANGE GINGERBREAD

2½ cups all-purpose flour
1½ tsps baking soda
½ tsp salt
1½ tsps ginger
½ tsp cinnamon
¼ tsp allspice
1 cup molasses
¼ lb (1 stick) butter or margarine, softened to room temperature
1 egg
½ cup (packed) brown sugar
½ cup unsweetened orange juice concentrate, undiluted
⅔ cup water

Topping:

1 pint (2 cups) heavy whipping cream
1½ Tbsps unsweetened orange juice concentrate, undiluted
1½ Tbsps sugar

Sift together flour, soda, salt and spices. Set aside. Combine molasses, softened butter, egg and sugar in a large mixing bowl. Beat with electric mixer on medium speed until very light and fluffy.

Place orange juice and water in a small saucepan. Heat until boiling. Alternately add small amounts of dry ingredients and juice mixture to molasses mixture. Beat on low speed with mixer until all have been added and mixed.

Grease and flour inside of a 13x9x2-inch Pyrex baking dish. Turn batter into dish, spreading top evenly. Bake in oven preheated to 350° for 40–45 minutes or until top springs back when lightly touched with finger. Cool in baking dish.

To make topping:

Combine cream, juice and sugar in a mixing bowl. Beat on medium speed until mixture holds shape. Cut gingerbread into squares. Swirl topping in center of each square.

BUTTONS AND BOWS DOUGHNUTS

2 Tbsps vegetable shortening
¾ cup sugar
2 eggs
4 cups all-purpose flour
2 tsps double-acting baking powder
½ tsp baking soda
½ tsp salt
½ tsp nutmeg
½ tsp lemon extract
1 cup buttermilk
oil for frying

Cream shortening and sugar in a mixing bowl and beat until light. Add eggs one at a time, beating well. Sift dry ingredients together. Mix extract and buttermilk. Alternately add dry ingredients and buttermilk mixture to shortening mixture, beating well after each addition.

Cover and place in refrigerator for 2 hours. Turn out on floured board or floured wax paper spread on counter. Pat down dough on board, then roll out to ½-inch thickness. Cut with floured doughnut cutter.

Remove center "buttons" from cut-out doughnuts. Holding one doughnut at a time, twist once across center to form "bows."

Fry in hot deep fat, turning once, until golden brown. Drain "buttons" and "bows" on absorbent paper. Sprinkle with powdered sugar, or glaze them. Makes about 2½ dozen.

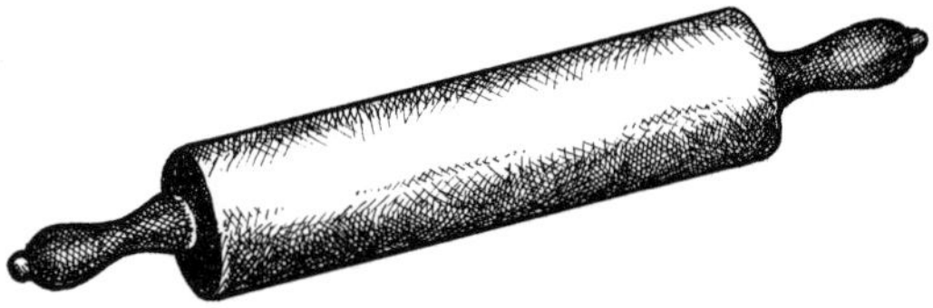

FLAKY PASTRY

Unbaked Pie Shell:

1⅓	cups all-purpose flour
⅔	tsp salt
½	cup all vegetable shortening
3 to 4	Tbsps ice water

Sift flour and salt together into a mixing bowl. Add shortening and cut in with a pastry blender until it is the texture of coarse cornmeal. Drizzle small amounts of water over mixture and stir well after each addition until all water is used. With hands, pack dough down well in the bowl. Form into a tight round ball.

Spread wax paper on a flat surface and flour lightly. Place dough in center of the paper. Flatten with hands until about ½ inch thick. Dust top lightly with flour and cover with wax paper. Roll out dough with rolling pin into a circle 12½ to 13 inches in diameter.

Remove top paper carefully. Lift pastry by bottom paper and turn into a 9-inch pie pan. Trim edges ½ inch out from rim of pan. Fold edges under until even with outer edge of pan rim. Flute edges all around. Makes 1 pie shell.

To keep rim of crust from over-browning when cooking pie in shell: Tear off several 2-inch-wide strips of foil. Arrange foil loosely but securely over and around rim of crust. Pour filling into crust and bake. Remove foil carefully after pie is done.

Baked Pie Shell:

Prepare Flaky Pastry as directed in Unbaked Pie Shell recipe. Prick inside of shell evenly all around and in center with a fork. Bake in oven preheated to 450° for 8–10 minutes or until it is a light golden brown.

MERINGUE TOPPING FOR PIES

3 egg whites
¼ tsp salt
dash cream of tartar
3 Tbsps sugar

Beat egg whites with an electric mixer until foamy. Add salt and cream of tartar. Slowly add sugar while beating constantly. Continue to beat until stiff peaks have formed.

Pile meringue in center of pie. Spread over pie filling and onto the edge of pie crust. Bake in oven preheated to 350° for 15 or 20 minutes or until lightly browned. Watch closely. Do not let meringue burn. Cool completely before cutting.

OLD-FASHIONED VANILLA PIE

2 cups milk
4 egg yolks
¾ cup sugar
4 tsps cornstarch
4 Tbsps sifted all-purpose flour
⅓ tsp salt
1½ Tbsps butter or margarine
1 tsp vanilla
One 9-inch Baked Pie Shell (see page 221)
Meringue Topping (see page 221)

Beat milk and egg yolks together until well blended. In the top of a double boiler, combine sugar, cornstarch, flour and salt. Mix well. Add egg mixture a little at a time, blending well with a spoon. Place pan over the bottom pan containing rapidly boiling water.

Over medium heat, add butter. Stirring thoroughly and constantly, cook until custard is very thick and smooth. Remove from heat and add vanilla. Stir well, scraping sides and bottom of pan until mixture is smooth.

Allow to cool only until meringue is prepared. Turn warm filling into the baked shell. Spread evenly with the back of a spoon. Pile meringue in the center of filling. Spread to rim of the crust. Bake in oven preheated to 350° for 15–18 minutes or until lightly and evenly browned on top. Allow pie to cool for 2 or 3 hours before cutting. Makes 6 to 8 portions.

Note: As a substitute for meringue, this pie may be topped with sweetened whipped cream. Let custard cool in crust before spreading with whipped cream. Refrigerate until chilled.

BLACK BOTTOM PIE

Old Fashioned Vanilla Pie filling (see page 222)
One 1-oz square unsweetened chocolate, melted

Prepare pie filling as recipe directs. Place ½ of the cooked mixture in a bowl. Add melted chocolate and mix well. Spread chocolate portion of filling into a baked pie shell. Spoon remaining filling over the chocolate one. Spread evenly.

While still hot, top with meringue and bake as directed in Old-Fashioned Vanilla Pie recipe. Or allow the pie to cool, then top with sweetened whipped cream.

BUTTERSCOTCH MERINGUE PIE

One 9-inch Baked Pie Shell (see page 221)
1 cup (packed) brown sugar
¼ cup cornstarch
½ tsp salt
1 cup water
1½ cups milk
3 egg yolks
1½ tsps vanilla
2 Tbsps butter, melted

Meringue:

3 egg whites
¼ tsp salt
⅓ cup brown sugar

Combine sugar, cornstarch and salt in a large saucepan. Mix thoroughly with the water. In a small mixing bowl, beat milk, egg yolks and vanilla together. Stir into sugar mixture.

Cook custard over medium heat, stirring vigorously and constantly until thickened. Remove from heat and add melted butter. Mix well. Return to heat. Cook and stir for 1 minute longer. Remove from heat and allow to cool somewhat while making Meringue.

Beat egg whites until foamy. Add salt and beat until soft peaks form. Beating constantly, add sugar slowly. Beat until stiff peaks form.

Spread warm butterscotch pie filling into baked shell. Pile meringue into center of pie. Spread with the back of a spoon, covering edge of crust. Bake in oven preheated to 350° for 15–20 minutes or until browned evenly. Remove from oven and cool for 2 or 3 hours before cutting. Makes 6 to 8 portions.

COCONUT MERINGUE PIE

One	9-inch Baked Pie Shell (see page 221)
¾	cup sugar
¼	cup cornstarch
½	tsp salt
2⅓	cups milk
3	egg yolks
1	tsp vanilla
2	Tbsps melted butter
1	cup flaked coconut
	Meringue Topping (see page 221)

Mix sugar, cornstarch and salt in a large saucepan. In a small mixing bowl, combine milk, egg yolks and vanilla. Beat until well mixed and frothy. Pour liquid into the saucepan. Stir well and place over medium heat.

Cook custard, stirring vigorously until mixture has thickened. Remove pan from heat and add butter and ¾ cup of the coconut. Blend well with a spoon. Return pan to medium heat. Continue to cook and stir for 1 minute. Remove from heat and set aside.

Make meringue according to recipe. Turn warm pie filling into baked pie shell. Spread evenly with the back of a spoon. Pile meringue in the center of filling. Spread to edge of crust. Sprinkle remaining ¼ cup coconut over top of meringue.

Bake in oven preheated to 350° for 15–20 minutes or until lightly browned. Take care not to burn. Cool pie for 2 or 3 hours before cutting. Makes 6 to 8 portions.

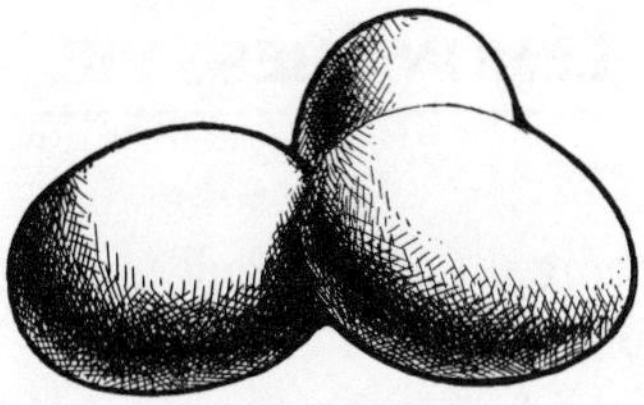

CHOCOLATE MERINGUE PIE

One 9-inch Baked Pie Shell (see page 221)
¾ cup sugar
4½ Tbsps cocoa, sifted
¼ cup cornstarch
½ tsp salt
2⅓ cups milk
3 egg yolks
3 Tbsps melted butter or margarine
1 tsp vanilla
Meringue Topping (see page 221)

Mix sugar, cocoa, cornstarch and salt in a large saucepan. In a small mixing bowl, combine milk, egg yolks and vanilla. Beat until well blended. Pour into saucepan with sugar mixture and stir well.

Cook custard over medium heat, stirring constantly and vigorously until thickened. Remove from heat and add butter. Stir well. Return to heat and cook 1 minute. Remove from heat and allow to cool slightly while making meringue.

When meringue is prepared, turn chocolate filling into pie shell. Spread evenly with the back of a spoon. Pile meringue in center of pie filling. With the back of a spoon, spread just over edge of crust.

Bake in oven preheated to 350° for 15–20 minutes or until lightly browned. Let pie cool for 2 or 3 hours before cutting. Makes 6 to 8 portions.

LEMON CHESS PIE

One 9- or 10-inch Unbaked Pie Shell (see page 220)
4 Tbsps butter or margarine
2 cups sugar
1 Tbsp all-purpose flour
2 Tbsps cornmeal
4 eggs
¼ cup half-and-half or evaporated milk
½ tsp vanilla
⅓ cup lemon juice

Preheat oven to 375°. Melt butter slowly in a small skillet over low heat.

Mix sugar, flour and cornmeal in a large mixing bowl. Add eggs and beat with a spoon. Stir in the half-and-half, melted butter, vanilla and lemon juice. Beat with an electric mixer on medium speed for 2 minutes.

Pour mixture into shell and place carefully on lower shelf in preheated oven. Bake for 15 minutes. Turn heat down to 325°. Bake for 35–40 minutes more. Allow pie to cool in pan before cutting. Serves 6.

Note: You may add ¼ cup chopped nuts, OR ¼ cup raisins, OR ¼ cup coconut to the filling just before pouring into pie shell.

SWEET POTATO PIE

2 large sweet potatoes or yams (about 1¼ lbs)
4 Tbsps melted butter
1 cup sugar
One 5⅓-oz can evaporated milk
3 Tbsps water
2 eggs, beaten
½ tsp cinnamon
¼ tsp nutmeg
¼ tsp salt
One 9-inch Unbaked Pie Shell (see page 220)

Cook potatoes in water until very tender. Drain and place in mixing bowl. Mash to a pulp with potato masher. Allow to cool to room temperature.

Stir in butter, sugar, milk and water. Add eggs, spices and salt. Beat with electric mixer until smooth.

Pour into unbaked pie shell. Place on heated baking sheet in center of oven preheated to 375°. Bake for 1 hour and 10 minutes or until knife inserted in center comes out clean.

Allow to cool for 2 or 3 hours before cutting. May be topped with whipped cream.

CHILLED STRAWBERRY PIE

One 9-inch Baked Pie Shell (see page 221)
2 cups thickly sliced fresh strawberries
¾ cup sugar
One 3-oz package strawberry-flavored gelatin
¾ cup boiling water
3 Tbsps cornstarch
¾ cup cold water
1 cup heavy cream, whipped

Combine strawberries and sugar in a bowl. Allow to stand 1 hour, stirring occasionally.

Mix ¾ cup boiling water with gelatin in a 2- or 3-quart saucepan. Stir until gelatin is dissolved completely.

Mix ¾ cup cold water with cornstarch. Pour into saucepan with gelatin. Cook and stir constantly over medium heat until thickened. Remove from heat and add strawberries, stirring well. Allow to cool to lukewarm.

Fold whipped cream into filling and spoon into pie shell. Chill for several hours before cutting. Makes 6 portions.

MINCEMEAT PIE

- 1⅔ cups (18-oz jar) prepared mincemeat
- 3 Tbsps brown sugar
- 3 Tbsps brandy
- 1½ cups peeled, cored and chopped apples
- ½ cup white raisins
- ½ cup chopped pecans or walnuts
- Double recipe of Flaky Pastry (see page 220)

Combine mincemeat, sugar and brandy in a mixing bowl. Stir thoroughly with a spoon. Add apples, raisins and nuts. Stir well.

Prepare pastry. Divide pastry. Roll out ½ on a floured board.

Line a 9-inch pie plate, leaving 1 inch of pastry over rim of pan.

Pour in filling and spread evenly with back of a spoon. Roll out remainder of pastry and arrange over top of pie. Trim edge and flute.

Make several vents on top crust with a knife and prick several times with a fork.

Bake in oven preheated to 425° for 15 minutes. Lower oven to 375°. Bake for 40 minutes more or until crust is golden.

CRUNCHY TOP APPLE PIE

3 lbs cooking apples
1 cup brown sugar
1 cup flour
¼ lb (1 stick) butter or margarine

Preheat oven to 350°. Grease inside of a 13x9x2-inch pan. Set aside.

Peel apples. Cut each into quarters. Remove cores. Cut each quarter into slices. Stack apples in pan and pack down.

Place butter in small skillet over low heat. Sift and measure flour and measure brown sugar by packing down in measuring cup. Mix flour and sugar. Combine flour mixture with melted butter. Mix thoroughly. Spread mixture over apples. Pack down with hands.

Bake for 1 hour. Remove pie from the oven and let cool for 1 hour. Good with a dab of whipped cream on top, but rich enough without it.

PECAN FUDGE PIE

One 9-inch Unbaked Pie Shell (see page 220)
4 Tbsps butter or margarine
Two 1-oz squares unsweetened chocolate
1 cup light corn syrup
3 large eggs
¾ cup sugar
1½ tsps vanilla
¼ tsp salt
1 cup coarsely chopped pecans
whipped cream (optional)

Melt butter and chocolate together in a small pan over low heat. Stir in syrup and remove pan from heat.

Combine eggs, sugar, vanilla and salt in a mixing bowl. Beat until well blended. Add butter mixture and pecans. Mix well, then pour into pie shell.

Bake in oven preheated to 350° for 45–50 minutes or until pie is barely set in center. Cool thoroughly before cutting. Serve plain or top with whipped cream. Makes 4 to 8 servings.

RAISIN AND SOUR CREAM PIE

1 cup seedless raisins
hot water
½ tsp cinnamon
⅛ tsp allspice
⅛ tsp ginger
½ cup (packed) brown sugar
½ cup white sugar
⅛ tsp salt
2 eggs

1 cup dairy sour cream
2 Tbsps lemon juice
One 9-inch Unbaked Pie Shell (see page 220)

Cover raisins with hot water and allow to soak for 5 minutes. Drain well and blot on paper towels.

Mix spices, sugars and salt together. Beat eggs in a mixing bowl until frothy. Add sour cream, lemon juice and sugar mixture. Stir until sugar dissolves. Add raisins and mix well.

Prick inside of pie shell with fork. Place in oven preheated to 400°. Bake for 6 minutes. Remove from oven and fill partially baked shell with pie filling. Reduce heat to 350°. Bake pie for 30–35 minutes. Cool completely before cutting. Better if chilled. Makes 6 servings.

COMPANY PUMPKIN PIE

1 cup light cream
3 eggs
¾ cup brown sugar
1 tsp cinnamon
¼ tsp nutmeg
⅛ tsp ginger
⅛ tsp allspice
¼ tsp salt
1¼ cups canned or cooked pumpkin (mashed)
One 9-inch Unbaked Pie Shell (see page 220)

Topping:

1 pint dairy sour cream
3 Tbsps maple syrup
2 Tbsps brown sugar
½ cup finely chopped pecans or walnuts

Combine cream, eggs, sugar, spices and salt in a large mixing bowl. Beat with electric mixer until well blended and frothy. Add pumpkin and mix well. Turn into unbaked pie shell. Bake in oven preheated to 350° for 1 hour or until done.

Remove pie (leave oven on) and let stand for 15 to 20 minutes. While pie is cooling somewhat, make Topping. Combine sour cream, syrup, sugar and ¼ cup of the nuts. Mix well with a spoon. Spread mixture over pie. Sprinkle remaining nuts over top. Return pie to oven for 10 minutes. Remove and allow to cool at room temperature. Chill in refrigerator for at least 3 hours.

PEANUT CHESS PIE

- 1 cup (packed) brown sugar
- ½ cup granulated sugar
- 1 Tbsp flour
- 2 eggs
- ¼ cup milk
- ¼ lb (1 stick) melted butter or margarine
- 1 cup shelled roasted peanuts, chopped
- 1 tsp vanilla
- One 9-inch Unbaked Pie Shell (see page 220)

Combine sugars and flour in a mixing bowl. Beat in eggs and milk. Add melted butter, peanuts and vanilla. Mix well. Turn into unbaked pie shell.

Bake in oven preheated to 375° for 40–45 minutes or until knife inserted in center of pie comes out clean. Cool thoroughly before cutting. Makes 6 to 8 portions.

PINEAPPLE BUTTERMILK PIE

1 cup sugar
¼ cup sifted all-purpose flour
¼ tsp salt
1 cup thick buttermilk
2 eggs
One 8¼-oz can crushed pineapple (less 1 Tbsp syrup reserved for topping)
½ tsp vanilla
One 8- or 9-inch Unbaked Pie Shell (see page 220)

Topping:

½ pt (1 cup) dairy sour cream
1 Tbsp syrup (reserved from pineapple)
3 Tbsps sugar

Combine sugar, flour and salt in a mixing bowl. Mix with spoon, mashing out any flour lumps with back of spoon. Stir in buttermilk, mixing well. Beat with an electric mixer on medium speed for 2 or 3 minutes, adding the eggs one at a time. Add pineapple and vanilla. Beat at medium speed for 2 or 3 minutes.

Turn into an 8- or 9-inch unbaked pie shell. Place in oven preheated to 400° for 25 minutes. Lower heat to 325° and bake for 30 minutes more. Remove from oven and let cool for 15 minutes.

Blend ingredients for topping and spread over pie filling. Return to oven preheated to 375° and bake for 10 minutes. Remove and allow to stand for 3 or 4 hours before cutting.

APPLE PUDDING WITH BRANDIED RAISIN SAUCE

1 cup brown sugar
4 Tbsps butter or margarine, softened
1 egg
¼ cup cream
1¼ cups flour
1 tsp baking soda
½ tsp cinnamon
⅛ tsp nutmeg
¼ tsp salt
2½ cups coarsely grated peeled and cored apples

Sauce:

1 cup cooked seedless raisins, drained
1 cup water
¼ cup sugar
2 Tbsps brandy
⅛ tsp salt
1 Tbsp cornstarch mixed with ¼ cup water

In a large mixing bowl, cream brown sugar and butter together. Add egg and cream, beating until well mixed and creamy. Sift flour, soda, cinnamon, nutmeg and salt together.

Combine dry ingredients with brown sugar mixture. Add grated apples and mix thoroughly. Turn into a greased 2-quart baking dish. Bake in oven preheated to 350° for 50–60 minutes.

To make sauce: Combine cooked raisins, water, sugar, brandy and salt in a saucepan. Bring mixture to a full boil over medium heat. Stir well and let boil for 1 minute. Add cornstarch/water mixture and stir constantly until thickened. Serve the pudding warm with hot raisin sauce on top. Serves 4 to 6.

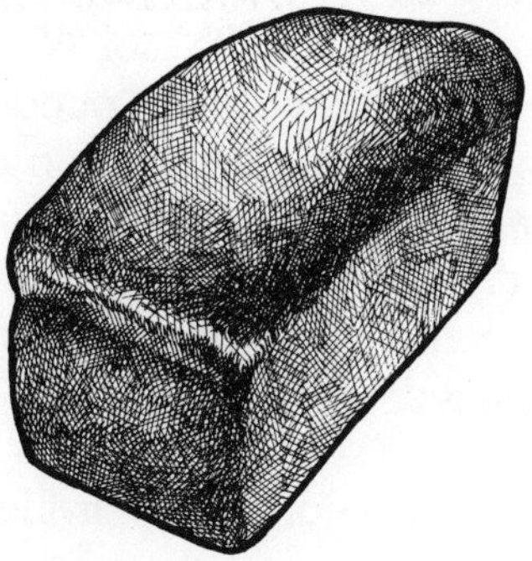

MERINGUE-TOPPED COUNTRY BREAD PUDDING

½ cup raisins
1 whole egg
5 egg yolks
4 cups milk
¾ cup sugar
1½ tsps vanilla
5⅓ Tbsps melted butter or margarine
4 cups finely cubed stale bread
½ cup chopped nuts

Topping:

5 egg whites
¼ tsp cream of tartar
½ cup sugar
nutmeg

Pour boiling water over raisins and allow to soak for 30 minutes. Drain, rinse well and drain again.

In a large mixing bowl, combine egg, egg yolks, 1 cup of the milk, sugar and vanilla. Beat on medium speed with an electric mixer until well blended. Add remaining 3 cups of milk and mix. Add butter, bread cubes, raisins and nuts. Stir well with a spoon.

Cover with plastic wrap and let stand for 20–30 minutes. Stir again and turn into a buttered 13x9x2-inch baking dish.

Bake in oven preheated to 325° for 45–50 minutes or until wooden toothpick inserted into center of pudding comes out clean.

To make topping: Beat egg whites with cream of tartar until soft peaks form. Continue beating and gradually add sugar. Beat until mixture holds stiff peaks. Spread meringue over hot pudding. Sprinkle top lightly with nutmeg. Return pudding to oven and bake until top is lightly browned. About 8 servings.

Note: Pudding may also be cooked in individual baking dishes.

MERINGUE-TOPPED CHOCOLATE PUDDING

- 1 whole egg
- 4 egg yolks
- 4 cups milk
- ¾ cup sugar
- 1 tsp vanilla
- 3 squares semisweet chocolate, melted
- 4 cups small cubes of dry bread
- ½ cup chopped nuts (optional)

Topping

- 4 egg whites
- ¼ tsp cream of tartar
- ⅓ cup sugar
- cocoa (optional)

Combine egg, egg yolks, 1 cup of the milk, sugar and vanilla in a large mixing bowl. Beat with electric mixer on medium speed until well blended. Add remaining 3 cups of the milk and melted chocolate. Beat until well mixed.

Add bread cubes and nuts, stirring well with a spoon. Cover

with plastic wrap and let stand for 20–30 minutes. Stir well again and turn into a buttered 13x9x2-inch Pyrex baking dish. Bake in oven preheated to 325° for 45–50 minutes or until wooden toothpick inserted in center of pudding comes out clean.

To make topping: Beat egg whites with cream of tartar until soft peaks form. Continue beating and add sugar gradually. Beat until stiff peaks form. Spread over hot pudding. Dust top lightly with cocoa. Return pudding to oven and bake until evenly browned. About 8 servings.

Note: Pudding may also be cooked in individual baking dishes.

COCONUT DATE MACAROONS

- 2 Tbsps flour
- 1/4 tsp salt
- 1/3 cup brown sugar
- 1 1/4 cups flaked coconut
- 2 egg whites
- 1/2 tsp vanilla
- 1/4 cup finely chopped pitted dates

Preheat oven to 325°. Grease a baking sheet and set aside.

Mix flour, salt and sugar together in a bowl. Add coconut and stir well. In another bowl, beat egg whites with a fork until they are foamy (do not beat too long). Add vanilla and mix.

Pour egg whites over coconut mixture. Stir and blend well until all of coconut is coated with egg whites. Add dates and mix well. Place one heaping teaspoon of the batter at a time on baking sheet, about 1 inch apart.

Place sheet in oven and bake for exactly 20 minutes. Allow macaroons to cool. Lift off sheet with a spatula. Makes about 30 macaroons.

CHOCOLATE OAT COOKIES

- 2 Tbsps flour
- ½ tsp salt
- ½ cup chopped nuts
- 1 cup old-fashioned rolled oats
- 2 egg whites
- ½ cup chocolate fudge topping (be sure it is not chocolate syrup)
- ½ tsp vanilla

Lightly grease a baking sheet. Preheat oven to 325°.

Combine flour, salt, nuts and oats in a bowl and mix well. In another bowl, beat egg whites with a fork until they are foamy (don't beat them too long). Add the fudge topping and vanilla to the egg whites and mix thoroughly.

Combine the egg mixture with the oat mixture. Stir and mix well, coating oats and nuts with the chocolate mixture. Place one heaping teaspoon of the batter at a time on the baking sheet, about 1 inch apart.

Place the sheet in the oven and bake for exactly 20 minutes. Let cookies cool in the pan. Loosen and lift cookies from the pan with a spatula. Makes about 30 cookies.

HOLIDAY COOKIES

¼ lb (1 stick) butter or margarine
One 8-oz package candied pineapple
One 8-oz package chopped candied cherries
One 8-oz package chopped pitted dates
1½ cups white raisins
2 cups chopped walnuts or pecans
¼ cup whiskey
1 cup (packed) brown sugar
2 eggs
1 tsp baking soda dissolved in 1 Tbsp buttermilk
1 tsp vanilla
1 tsp almond extract
½ tsp cinnamon
½ tsp nutmeg
1¾ cups flour

Place butter in a large mixing bowl and allow to soften at room temperature. In another bowl, place pineapple, cherries, dates, raisins and nuts. Drizzle whiskey over all. Stir well with a spoon. Allow to soak, stirring occasionally.

Pour sugar into bowl with butter. Cream the two together with a spoon. Add eggs and beat until mixed evenly. Add soda dissolved in buttermilk, extracts, cinnamon and nutmeg.

Gradually add the flour, mixing well. Add fruit and nuts. Stir until mixed thoroughly.

Drop one heaping teaspoon for each cookie on greased baking sheet. Allow 1½ inches between cookies. Bake in oven preheated to 325° for 10–12 minutes or until lightly browned. Remove each with a spatula to wax paper spread on counter. Cool thoroughly before storing in cookie jar. Makes 75 to 100 cookies.

MAMA'S OATMEAL COOKIES

1 cup shortening (not oil)
1 cup (packed) brown sugar
¾ cup white sugar
2 eggs, beaten
2 tsps vanilla
¼ tsp cinnamon
1 tsp soda
1 tsp salt
1½ cups flour
3 cups old-fashioned rolled oats
1 cup chopped nuts

In a large mixing bowl, cream shortening and sugars until smooth. Add eggs, vanilla, cinnamon, soda and salt. Beat until evenly mixed.

Add flour, then oats and nuts, mixing thoroughly after each addition.

Roll into balls about 1 inch in diameter. Press down in center to flatten slightly. Bake in oven preheated to 325° on greased baking sheets for 10–12 minutes or until lightly browned.

Remove with a spatula to wax paper on counter. Allow to cool for 1 hour before storing. Makes 60–75 cookies.

FRUIT

BANANA FRITTERS

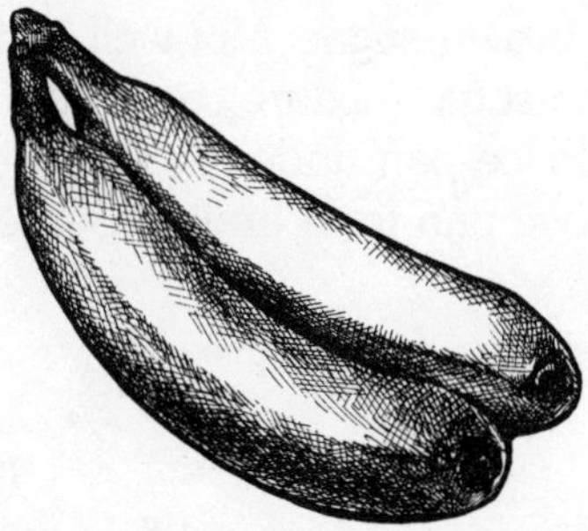

6 large firm bananas
1 cup flour
¼ tsp salt
3 Tbsps sugar
¾ cup milk
1 egg yolk
¼ tsp vanilla
1 egg white
cooking oil
powdered sugar

Peel bananas and cut in half lengthwise. Cut each half in two crosswise.

Sift flour, salt and sugar together. In a mixing bowl, combine milk, egg yolk and vanilla. Beat until egg is mixed. Add dry ingredients slowly, beating constantly.

Beat egg white until high peaks form. Fold into batter in mixing bowl.

Heat 3 inches of oil in a deep fryer or skillet until very hot, but not smoking. Dip each piece of banana one at a time into batter and drop into hot fat. Do not overcrowd, cook only a few at a time.

When golden brown, place on absorbent paper to drain. Sprinkle with powdered sugar. Serves 6.

NUTTY GRILLED BANANAS

6 ripe bananas
1/3 cup brown sugar
3 Tbsps butter or margarine
1/4 cup finely chopped nuts

Turn oven setting to broil. Peel bananas and cut each in half lengthwise. Select a pan (not glass) that banana halves will fit into side by side. Place in pan round sides down, cut sides up.

Place brown sugar in bowl. Melt butter over low heat and pour over brown sugar. Mix well. Add chopped nuts. Mix thoroughly. Spoon sugar mixture carefully on top of bananas.

Place pan under broiler. Cook until topping starts to bubble. Remove pan from broiler. Serves 6.

GLAZED STRAWBERRIES

3 pints ripe strawberries
1 cup sugar
3/4 cup water

Wash berries and discard stems. Turn out on a towel and dry thoroughly.

Combine sugar and water in a saucepan. Bring to a boil over medium heat, stirring until sugar dissolves. Cook until mixture forms a very thin ribbon when dropped from a spoon.

With a slotted spoon, dip 2 or 3 berries at a time into syrup, then place in a serving bowl. Continue dipping berries until each has been coated. Serve with thick cream. Makes 6 portions.

FIGS IN SYRUP

2 lbs fresh very ripe figs
1½ cups sugar
1½ cups water
3 Tbsps lemon juice

Wash figs thoroughly. Cut off and discard stem ends. Plunge in a large pot of boiling water. Cook 2 minutes and drain. Add fresh cool water to cover well. Boil until figs are almost tender. Drain.

Add sugar, water and lemon juice to figs. Cook and stir until syrup has thickened and figs are tender. Chill. Serve for breakfast with thick cream.

AMBROSIA

juice from mandarin oranges as directed
coconut milk as directed
3 Tbsps sugar
2 tsps cornstarch
1 medium fresh coconut, grated
Two 11-oz cans mandarin oranges, well drained
2 tsps poppy seed

Combine juice from mandarin oranges and coconut milk to measure 1¼ cups. Pour into saucepan. Stir in sugar and cornstarch. Cook and stir constantly over medium heat until thickened. Allow to cool.

Place grated coconut and orange segments in a mixing bowl. Stir in sauce and poppy seed. Blend well with a spoon. Turn into a serving bowl, cover and chill. Serves 6.

Note: Pineapple tidbits may be added to this recipe.

SPICED PEACHES

1 large can peach halves
½ cup sugar
½ cup corn syrup
¼ cup white vinegar
½ tsp whole cloves
Several pieces cinnamon stick

Pour the juice from peaches into a 2-quart saucepan. Add sugar, syrup, vinegar and spices. Place over medium heat and allow juice to boil. Cook and stir occasionally for a few minutes.

Arrange peach halves in a quart jar. Pour hot mixture over peaches. Cool, then refrigerate for a few hours before serving.

POACHED PEACHES AND PEARS

3 large fresh ripe peaches (or apricots)
3 large fresh ripe pears
1½ cups hot water
3 Tbsps brandy
1 cup sugar
½ tsp allspice

Peel fresh peaches (or apricots) and halve carefully. Remove and discard pits. Peel pears and cut in half. Remove cores.

Combine water, brandy, sugar and allspice in a saucepan. Bring to a boil over medium heat. Cook and stir until sugar dissolves.

Arrange fruit in a wide pot and pour syrup over top. Place over medium heat. Cook and stir occasionally for 10 minutes. Serve hot or cold. Serves 6.

MINT PEARS

- 6 large fresh ripe pears
- 1 cup sugar
- 1¼ cups water
- 4 drops peppermint or spearmint extract
- ½ tsp green food coloring

Peel pears and cut in half. Remove cores carefully. Combine sugar and water in a saucepan. Cook and stir until sugar has dissolved. Remove from heat and add extract and coloring. Mix well.

Arrange pears side by side and cut side up in a large skillet. Pour colored syrup over pears. Place over medium heat.

Cook and stir occasionally for 5 minutes. Turn pears cut side down. Cook and stir until syrup has thickened somewhat. Good served with lamb. Serves 6.

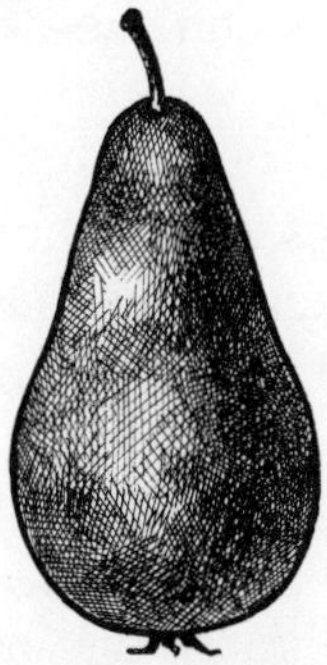

CINNAMON PEARS

1 large can pear halves in heavy syrup
2 cinnamon sticks, each broken into 3 or 4 pieces
½ tsp red food coloring

Drain syrup from pears into a saucepan. Add cinnamon sticks. Place pan over medium heat and allow syrup to come to a boil. Remove from burner. Add coloring to syrup and stir well with spoon.

Arrange pears in a quart jar. Pour liquid over pears. Allow to cool. Screw lid on jar and place in refrigerator overnight so fruit will take on red color and cinnamon flavor. Pretty at Christmastime and for company dinners.

CHEESE-BATTERED PINEAPPLE RINGS

8 to 12 slices canned pineapple (allow 2 per person)
2 eggs
½ cup pineapple juice
¼ tsp salt
1 Tbsp sugar
½ cup all-purpose flour
¼ cup grated American cheese
light cooking oil

Drain pineapple slices well and place on paper towels to blot. Set aside. In a small mixing bowl beat eggs, juice, salt and sugar together until frothy. Add flour and cheese. Beat with a spoon until well blended.

Pour oil ½ inch deep into a skillet. Heat to sizzling over medium heat. With tines of fork inserted in the hole in center of each pineapple slice, dip slices, one at a time, into the batter and place in hot oil in skillet.

Cook about 4 slices at a time so as not to crowd. Turn when lightly browned on bottom and cook other sides. Drain well on absorbent paper. Keep hot in warm oven. Good as a garnish for roasts, chicken, steaks and chops. Serves 4 to 6.

BAKED APPLES

6 baking apples (Rome Beauty is the best type)
6 tsps brown sugar

Preheat oven to 375°. Wash, dry and core the apples. Place 1 teaspoon brown sugar in center of each apple. Wrap apples separately in foil. Bake apples for 50–60 minutes or until they are done. Serve with heavy cream. Serves 6.

BAKED APPLES STUFFED WITH PRUNES

6 apples
pitted prunes
6 tsps sugar
½ tsp cinnamon

Prepare apples as for Baked Apples. Roll each prune in mixture of sugar and cinnamon. Stuff as many prunes as the core holes in the apples will hold.

Bake in foil as directed in preceding recipe. Serves 6.

Note: Fresh, frozen or canned pitted dark sweet (Bing) cherries may be substituted for the prunes.

SPICED APPLES

3	lbs red cooking apples
½	cup water
½	cup sugar
½	tsp cinnamon
⅛	tsp allspice
⅛	tsp salt
2 or 3	drops red food coloring (optional)

Core and peel apples. Cut each into 8 wedges. Set aside.

Combine all other ingredients in a pot. Over medium heat, cook and stir until sugar dissolves. Add apples, stirring to coat with liquid.

Bring to a boil. Reduce heat to low and cover with lid. Cook and stir occasionally until apples are barely tender (apples will turn to mush if overcooked). Serve hot or cold.

Spiced Apples keep well in the refrigerator.

CRAN-APPLE SAUCE

4	cooking apples
1	lb fresh cranberries
2	cups sugar
2½	cups water
⅛	tsp salt

Peel and core apples. Cut into chunks about ¾ inch square. Wash cranberries thoroughly.

Place sugar, water and salt in a pot. Allow to boil 2 or 3 minutes. Add apples and cranberries. Cook until apples are tender and skins of cranberries pop open, about 15 minutes. Remove from heat. May be served hot or cold. Makes about 5 cups.

CRANBERRY RELISH

1 lb fresh cranberries
1½ cups sugar
¼ cup apple, pineapple or orange juice
2 Tbsps lemon juice
2 cups chopped celery
2 cups chopped apples
½ cup white raisins

Wash cranberries thoroughly. Put through coarse blade of food chopper. Combine cranberries, sugar and juices in pot and place over high heat. Stir well and allow to come to a boil. Cook and stir 2 or 3 minutes.

Allow cranberries to cool thoroughly. Add celery, apples and raisins. Stir well. Store in a covered jar in refrigerator. Makes about 5 cups.

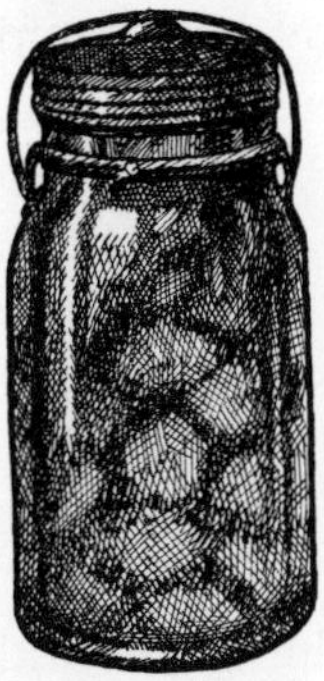

MIXED DRIED FRUITS IN SYRUP

1 to 2 lbs mixed dried fruits
water for soaking as directed
1½ cups sugar
2 to 2½ cups water
¼ tsp allspice
⅛ tsp salt

Wash fruit and place in a large pot. Pour enough cool water over fruit to cover by 3 to 4 inches. Allow to soak overnight.

Drain off soaking water. Add all other ingredients to fruit. Bring to a rolling boil over high heat. Lower heat to medium. Cook until fruit is tender and syrup has thickened.

Good with heavy cream for breakfast. Serves 6.

Note: Any dried fruit may be substituted for the mixed fruit—pears, peaches, apples, prunes, raisins, and so on. Use less sugar with raisins.

FRUIT COMPOTE

- 1 cup fruit juice (orange, pineapple)
- ¼ cup sugar
- 1 Tbsp cornstarch
- 1 tsp rum or brandy
- 1 large ripe cantaloupe
- 1 pint (2 cups) fresh or frozen whole strawberries
- 2 bananas, peeled and sliced
- 2 cups pineapple tidbits (fresh, frozen or canned)

Combine juice, sugar, cornstarch and rum in a saucepan. Cook and stir constantly over medium heat until thickened. Set aside.

Remove and discard rind, seed and membranes from melon. Cut cantaloupe meat into bite-size pieces. If strawberries are fresh, wash thoroughly and discard stems.

Combine cantaloupe chunks, sliced bananas, pineapple tidbits and strawberries in a mixing bowl. Add cooled sauce. Stir to coat all pieces.

Cover and refrigerate. Serves 6.

Note: Watermelon is very good in a compote. Other fruits may also be substituted or added such as seedless grapes, apples, navel oranges, nectarines, etc.

APRICOT JAM

4	lbs fully ripe apricots
1/3	cup water
1	Tbsp lemon juice
One	1¾-oz jar powdered pectin
7	cups sugar
	paraffin, melted

Peel apricots and remove pits. Chop fruit coarsely. Combine prepared fruit, water, lemon juice and pectin in a 6-quart pot. Stir thoroughly.

Over high heat, bring mixture to a rolling boil, stirring constantly. Add sugar all at once. Stir and cook until sugar melts. When mixture returns to a full rolling boil, cook for 2 or 3 minutes, stirring constantly.

Remove from heat. Skim off and discard foam. Ladle fruit into hot sterilized jars. Pour melted paraffin ⅛ to ¼ inch thick over fruit in each jar. Place caps loosely on jar and allow to cool.

When jars have cooled to room temperature, screw lids on tightly. Makes 5 pints or 10 half-pints.

Note: It may take 1 or 2 weeks for Apricot Jam to gel. Store in a cool place for 2 or 3 weeks before opening a jar.

BRANDIED PEACH PRESERVES

3½	lbs fully ripe peaches, peeled and pitted
¼	cup water
1	Tbsp lemon juice
2	Tbsps brandy
One	1¾-oz box powdered pectin
5½	cups sugar
	paraffin, melted

Cut peeled and pitted peaches into pieces about ½ inch square. Place in a 6-quart pot. Combine water, juice and brandy. Mix with fruit. Add pectin and stir thoroughly to blend.

Place over high heat and stir constantly. Cook for 1 minute after mixture comes to a hard, rolling boil.

Add sugar all at once. Stir vigorously until sugar dissolves. Bring to a rolling boil again and cook 2 or 3 minutes, stirring constantly. Remove from heat. Skim off and discard foam.

Ladle mixture into hot sterilized jars. Pour melted paraffin ⅛ to ¼ inch thick over fruit in jars. Place lids loosely on jars. When cooled to room temperature, screw lids down tightly. Makes 4 pints or 8 half-pints.

WATERMELON RIND PRESERVES

3 quarts watermelon rind (measure after preparing as below)
water as directed
salt as directed
9 cups sugar
3 Tbsps lemon juice
1 cinnamon stick
2 tsps whole cloves
paraffin, melted

Use only the white part of the watermelon between the red meat and thin outer green part. Cut rind into 1½x¾-inch pieces. Place in large crock or enamel or glass container.

Mix 1 gallon of water and ½ cup salt. Stir until salt dissolves. Pour over pieces of rind. If not enough water to cover, make more brine and add. Soak rind overnight.

Next day, drain off brine. Cook watermelon rind in fresh water until barely tender. Drain thoroughly. Measure 3 quarts rind at this point.

Combine sugar, lemon juice, cinnamon stick, cloves and 2 quarts of water in a very large pot. Bring to a full boil over high heat. Boil for 5 minutes. Remove spices. Add rind.

Cook until rind is clear and syrup has thickened. Remove from heat. Skim off and discard foam. Ladle preserves into sterilized jars.

Pour melted paraffin over preserves in jar to a thickness of ⅛ to ¼ inch. Place lids loosely on jars. When cool, screw tops tightly and store.

Makes about 8 pints or 16 half-pints.

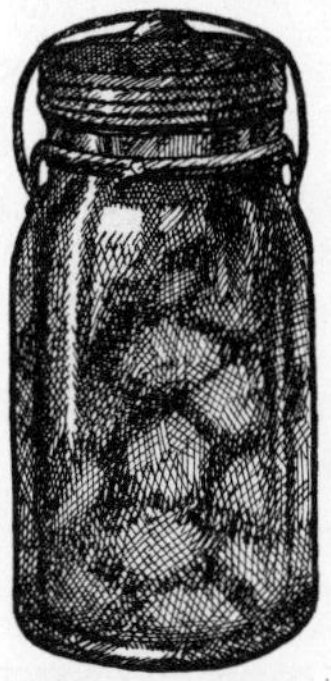

FIG PRESERVES

- 3½ lbs fully ripe figs
- boiling water as directed
- 1½ cups water
- ½ cup lemon juice
- One 1¾-oz box powdered pectin
- 7½ cups sugar
- paraffin, melted

Wash figs, cut off and discard stem ends. Plunge fruit into a pot of boiling water (enough to cover). Allow to boil 5 minutes. Drain and rinse in cool water. Cut each fig into about 8 pieces.

Combine figs, 1½ cups water and lemon juice in a 6- or 8-quart pot. Bring to a boil over high heat. Reduce heat and simmer, uncovered, for 15 minutes, stirring often. Remove from heat and allow to cool.

Stirring constantly, add pectin slowly. Return to heat and bring to a hard boil. Add sugar, stirring well. Bring to a full rolling boil and cook 1 minute, stirring constantly.

Remove from heat. Skim off and discard foam. Ladle into hot jars leaving ½ inch at top. Wipe rims dry down to top of fruit. Pour melted paraffin ⅛ to ¼ inch thick into each jar over fruit. Place lids on jars, but do not screw down. Allow to cool, then screw down lids tightly.

Store in a cool place. Makes about 11 half-pints.

CANTALOUPE PRESERVES

2 lbs prepared cantaloupe (weigh after reading directions)
4 cups sugar
2 Tbsps lemon juice

Peel melon and cut crosswise into 1-inch-thick slices. Scoop out seeds and membranes in center of each piece. Cut slices into ¾-inch widths.

Weigh prepared melon pieces to measure 2 pounds. Place in a large bowl and mix with sugar. Cover and refrigerate for 16–18 hours. Add lemon juice.

Transfer mixture to a 6-quart pot. Boil until melon pieces are clear. While still boiling hot, ladle into hot sterilized jars. Seal at once. Makes 6 to 8 half-pints.

TOMATO PRESERVES

2½ lbs ripe red tomatoes
2 Tbsps lemon juice
¼ cup water
One 1¾-oz box powdered pectin
4½ cups sugar
paraffin, melted

Scald tomatoes one at a time and peel. Cut out stems and discard. Cut tomatoes into pieces about 1 inch in length. Place in a 6-quart pot. Combine lemon juice and water. Pour over tomatoes. Add pectin. Stir well to blend.

Place over high heat and bring to a full rolling boil. Boil for 1 minute. Add sugar all at once. Stir constantly as mixture returns to a full boil. Cook 2 or 3 minutes, stirring constantly.

Remove pot from heat. Skim off and discard foam. Ladle tomato mixture into hot sterilized jars. Pour melted paraffin ⅛ to ¼ inch deep on top of preserves. Place lids loosely on tops.

When cooled to room temperature, screw lids tightly in place. Makes 6 to 7 half-pints.

INDEX

A

B

C

D

E

F

R

S

Y

Z